Mystic Shawls

Anna Dalvi

Cooperative Press
Cleveland, Ohio

Mystic Shawls

ISBN 13 (print): 978-1-937513-54-2

ISBN 13 (e-book): 978-1-937513-55-9

First Edition

Published by Cooperative Press

http://www.cooperativepress.com

Patterns © 2014, Anna Dalvi

Photos © 2014, Caro Sheridan

Model: Rebecca Patterson

Every effort has been made to ensure that all the information in this book is accurate at the time of publication; however, Cooperative Press neither endorses nor guarantees the content of external links referenced in this book.

If you have questions or comments about this book, or need information about licensing, custom editions, special sales, or academic/corporate purchases, please contact Cooperative Press: info@cooperativepress.com or 13000 Athens Ave C288, Lakewood, OH 44107 USA

For Cooperative Press

Senior Editor: Shannon Okey

Acquisitions / Assistant Editor: MK Carroll

Art Director / Copy Editor: Elizabeth Green Musselman

Book Designer: Kayt de Fever

To Aneesh,
Linnea, Axel & Viggo,
With love.

contents

introduction

If you've spent any time at all on the internet—around Ravelry, craft blogs, or the like—you've probably heard people talking about KALs. A KAL is simply shorthand for a Knit-ALong, as in a group of people who are knitting something particular at the same time. Each person knits their own project, and along the way they chat, share pictures, and cheer on each other's progress.

What exactly is being knit depends on the format of the KAL. Often a knitalong is set up for people knitting the same pattern, but sometimes it is organized around a theme, like "knit a pair of socks," or "knit a triangular lace shawl," or "knit something by designer X," or really any theme you can think of.

Mystery KALs are a little different. A mystery KAL is usually hosted by a designer, and the people who participate have only a vague idea of what the final product will look like. The type of project is known—it might be a lace shawl, for example—as are the type and amount of yarn. Sometimes there are color suggestions included, and sometimes you will know the "theme" of the design up front.

The first time I heard about mystery KALs was back in 2007. A friend of mine had joined one and suggested that I join along with her. I wasn't at all sure what to expect. The KAL was for a lace stole, and we were going to get weekly "clues" to knit

from. There was going to be one new clue each week for five weeks.

I wondered how this would work. Was my first clue going to be "cast on enough stitches to make a 45 cm wide stole and then knit in a leaf pattern until the stole measures 30 cm and then wait for the next clue"?

Luckily, this is not at all how mystery KALs work; at least, not any that I have ever participated in (although now that I think about it, that might be a lot of fun). The weekly clues are actually just a portion of the pattern. So for the first week, you might get the setup instructions and the first part of the pattern. The next week you will get a little bit more and so on, until the last week when you get the last part of the pattern, including bind-off and finishing instructions.

That first mystery KAL that I participated in was a lot of fun. I eagerly knitted up each part of the pattern every week and then waited for the next clue to be released. It was thrilling to see the lace developing and try to predict what might be next.

Once the KAL finished, I started looking around for another one to join immediately. Unfortunately, I couldn't seem to find one. So I thought: why don't I just design my own lace shawl and offer it as a mystery KAL? Really, how hard could it be?

Now, at that time I hadn't actually published a single pattern yet, even though I did have a design accepted by an upcoming publication. So I was a complete unknown. But I figured that maybe if I could get 20 people or so to join my little mystery KAL, that would be fun. So I cast on, and after knitting more than half of my shawl, I opened "sign-ups" on my blog and set the starting date for four weeks off in the future, so that I would have plenty of time to finish the shawl before the KAL started—and lots of time to try to find someone who might want to join. I called my new design Mystic Waters and wrote a little description to try to entice people:

Have you ever found yourself staring into a deep ocean pondering the mysteries beneath the surface?

Or swam in a dark lake at sunset?

Do you feel the lightness of the summer rain?

Water has many forms and faces, and yet they are all the same—simple H2O.

The response was overwhelming. Not only did I get the 20 or so people I had been hoping for—more than 1,400 knitters worldwide signed up to join my mystery KAL.

Once my first mystery KAL was over, I immediately hosted another one. And then another one.... Over the years, I have hosted many, and they have always been made up of a great group of knitters. The format has varied—from large shawls with weekly clues, to smaller shawls published as a mystery—but the knitter receives the entire pattern at once, on a specified date.

This book contains all the Mystic patterns published to date. In a way, they chronicle the first six years of my design career. Throughout the book you will see pictured not only my own samples of these patterns, but also beautiful examples that other knitters created during the knitalongs. The mix of photographs not only hints at the infinite possibilities contained in a single pattern, but also displays the glorious artistic community that you can find in KALs.

Clockwise from top left:
Mystic Embers, Mystic Air,
Mystic Light and Mystic Star.

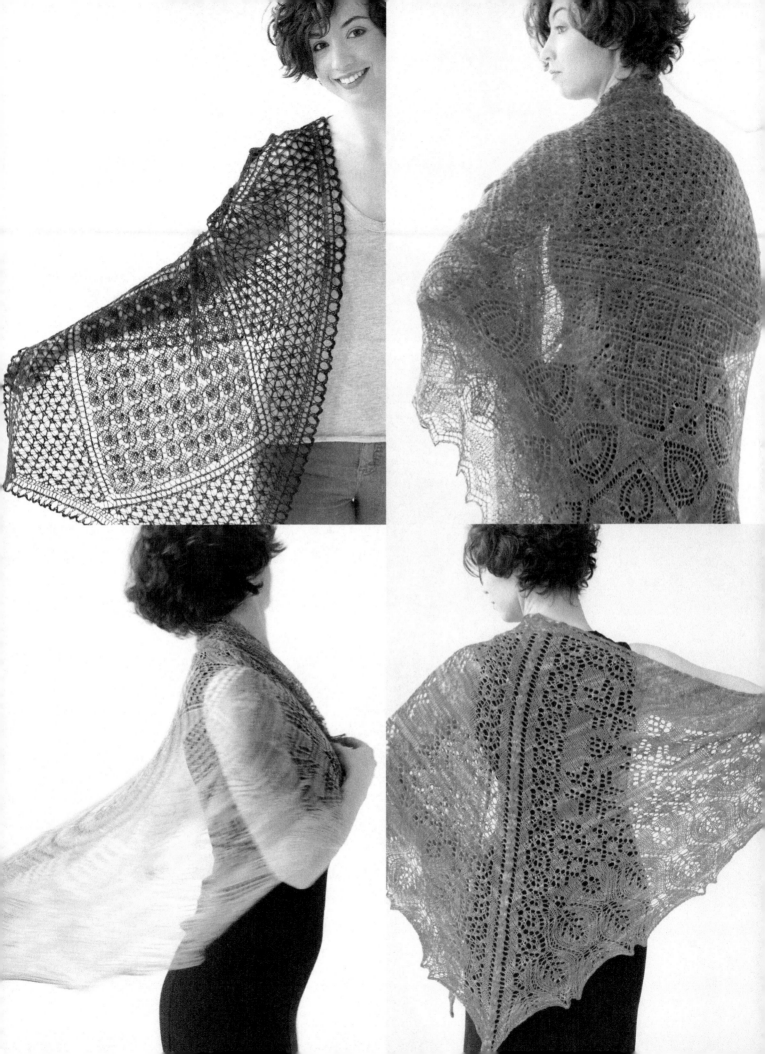

mystic waters

Have you ever found yourself staring into a deep ocean pondering the mysteries beneath the surface? Or swam in a dark lake at sunset? Do you feel the lightness of the summer rain?

Water has many forms and faces, and yet they are all the same—simple H_2O.

Mystic Waters was my first mystic knit-along. It was also the first lace shawl I ever designed.

When knitting lace, it is very important to pay attention to the edges. If the cast-on and bound-off edges are too tight, the piece puckers unpleasantly, so I decided to minimize the potential trouble-areas.

The shawl starts with a cast on of just two stitches, which form the bottom point of the triangle. The triangle then grows, row by row, until you reach a surprise at the end: the shawl is not bound off in one straight edge. Instead, you knit a border across the top and bind off only 6 stitches, which matches the width of the border.

The motifs are meant to show water in its various forms. Along the outside of the triangle are stacked frost patterns. Then there are water droplets. At bottom center, the pattern shows the frothing water you'd see as waves break against the shore. Above that are some waves, and then water falling as if from a waterfall. Across the top lie snowflakes—water's frozen state.

The obvious color to use for Mystic Waters is of course blue. And there were many people who chose to knit their shawls in blue. But others reasoned that water can be white, like snow. Or green. Or why not even red as when it's reflecting the setting sun?

The Mystic Waters KAL brought together knitters from all over the world. The knit-along was advertised on my blog, and people who joined blogged about their progress. There was a blog badge and banner created that people could add to their blogs to create some visual unity.

Elaine, Driftwood, TX

9

Mystic Waters

MATERIALS

2 skeins of Fårö from Klippan [100% merino – 600 yds/549 m per 100 g] or similar yarn

3.75 mm [US 5] needles

Large-eyed, blunt needle

GAUGE

15 sts and 30 rows = 4 in [10 cm] in stockinette stitch, blocked

FINISHED (BLOCKED) SIZE

Large: width: 250 cm [98"], height: 128 cm [50"]

Small: width: 180 cm [71"], height: 97 cm [38"]

INSTRUCTIONS

CO 2 sts using the long-tail cast on.
Setup row 1 (WS): Kfb twice [4 sts].

Then continue with the charts. Only the RS rows are charted. Rows are read from right to left.
Each WS row is worked as follows: K2, purl to the last 2 sts, k2.

If knitting the larger size, knit all rows on Charts A–J.

Do NOT work a WS row after row 367, and do NOT break the yarn.

If knitting the smaller size, knit rows 1–263 on Charts A–E (not rows 265–7 on Chart E) and the special Chart F for the smaller size only. Do NOT work a WS row after row 289 for the smaller size shawl.

FINISHING INSTRUCTIONS

At this point, CO an additional 5 sts (by knitting them on).

Row 1 (WS): K5, p2tog; turn work.
Row 2 (RS): Sl1, k5.

Row 3: K2, p3, p2tog.
Row 4: Sl1, k1, k2tog, yo, k2.

Rep rows 3–4 until 1 unworked stitch remains.

Row 5: K5, p2tog; turn work.
Row 6: Sl1, k5.

BO 6 sts.

Sew in ends and block.

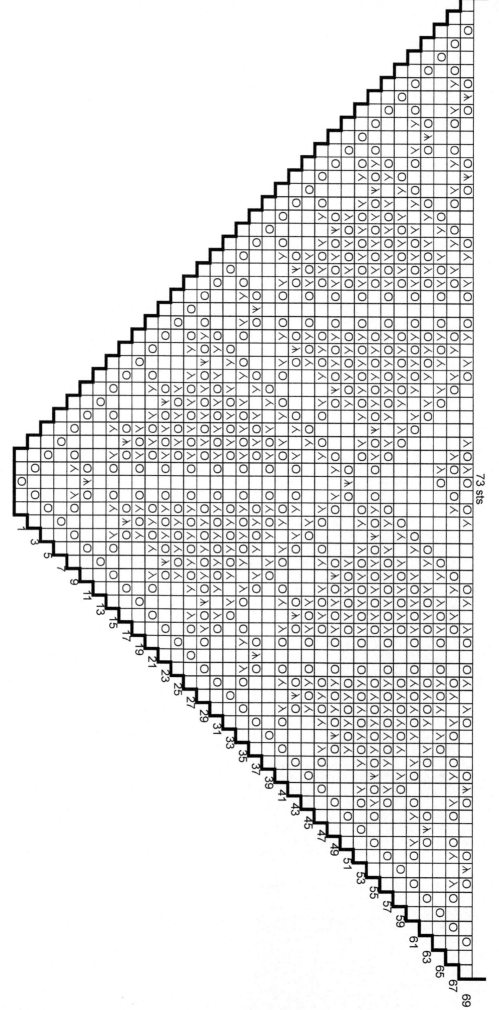

Mystic Waters – CHART A

73 sts

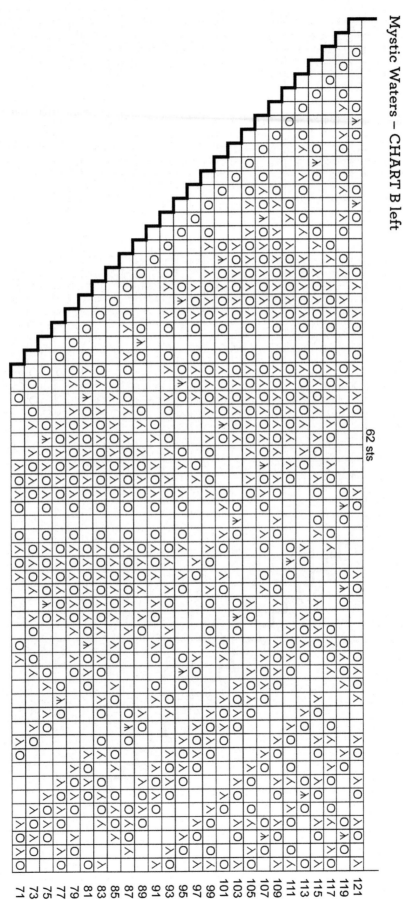

62 sts

(Right half of chart B continues from here.)

13

(Left half of chart B continues from here.)

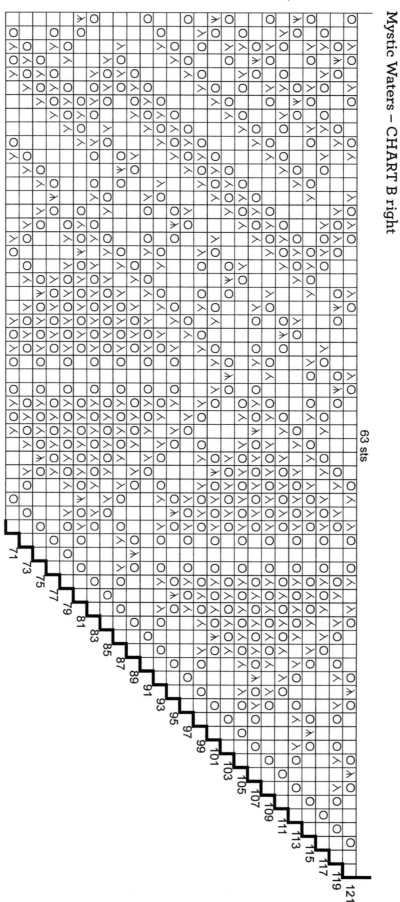

63 sts

(Left half of chart C continues from here.)

Mystic Waters – CHART C right

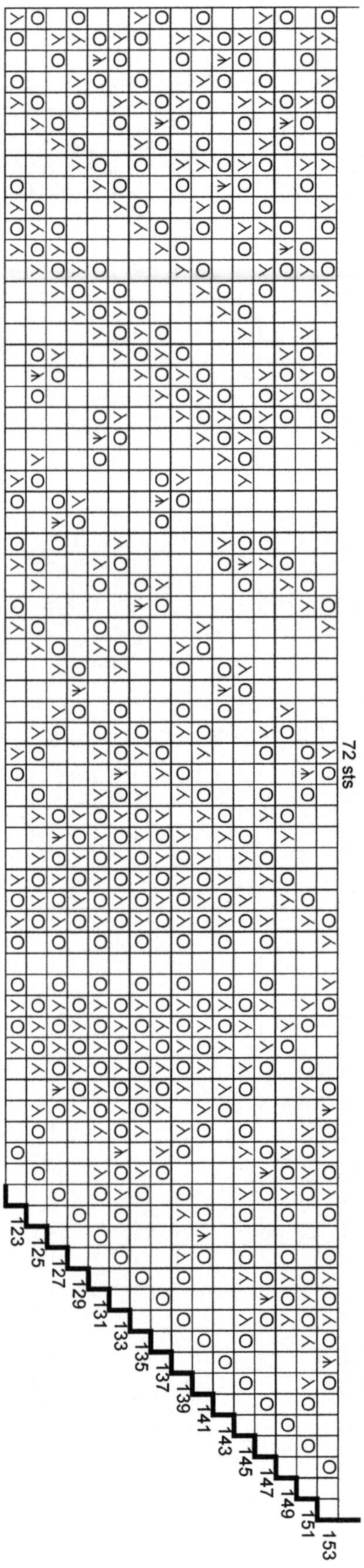

Mystic Waters – CHART C left

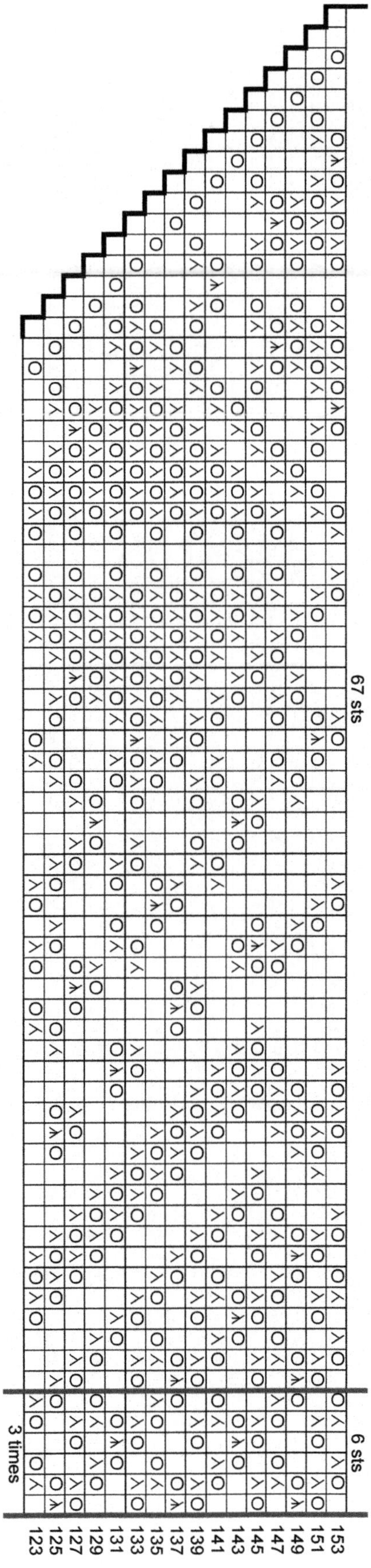

72 sts

67 sts

6 sts

3 times

(Right half of chart C continues from here.)

(Left section of chart D continues from here.)

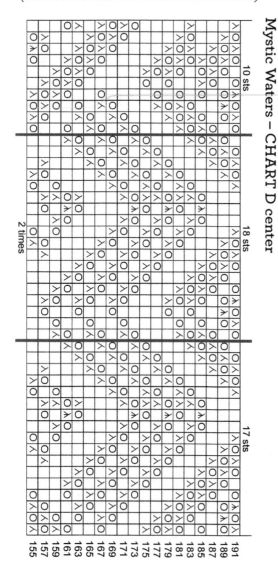

Mystic Waters – CHART D center

10 sts

18 sts

2 times

17 sts

155 157 159 161 163 165 167 169 171 173 175 177 179 181 183 185 187 189 191

(Right section of chart D continues from here.)

Mystic Waters – CHART D left

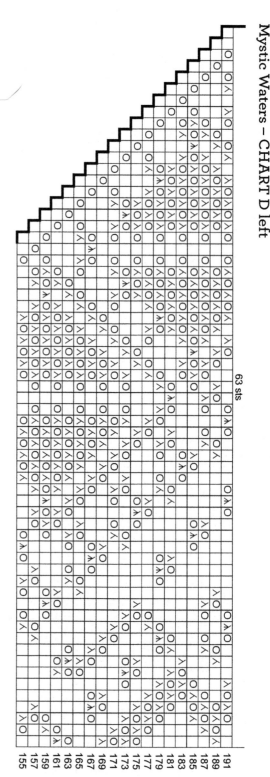

63 sts

155 157 159 161 163 165 167 169 171 173 175 177 179 181 183 185 187 189 191

(Center of chart D continues from here.)

(Center of chart D continues from here.)

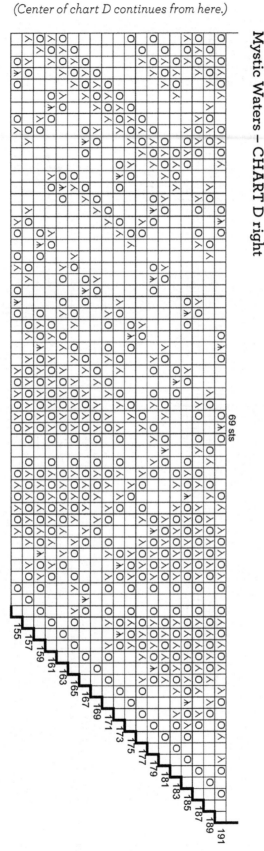

69 sts

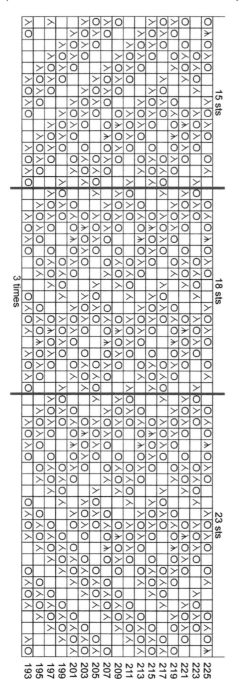

(Left section of chart E continues from here.)

Mystic Waters – CHART E left

Mystic Waters – CHART E center

15 sts

18 sts

3 times

23 sts

68 sts

193 195 197 199 201 203 205 207 209 211 213 215 217 219 221 223 225

(Right section of chart E continues from here.)

(Center of chart E continues from here.)

(Center of chart E continues from here.)

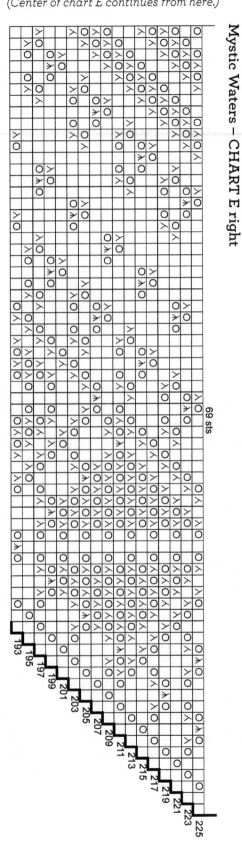

Mystic Waters – CHART E right

69 sts

193 195 197 199 201 203 205 207 209 211 213 215 217 219 221 223 225

(Left section of chart F continues from here.)

Mystic Waters – CHART F center

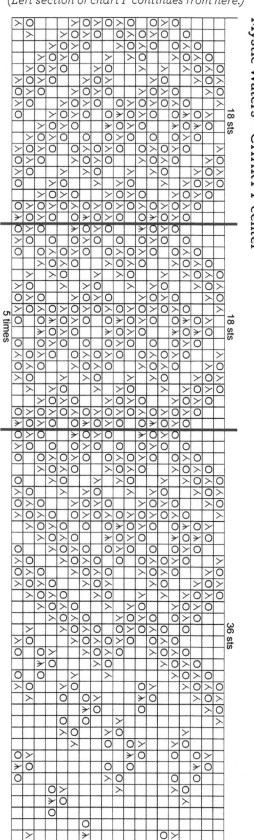

18 sts

5 times

18 sts

36 sts

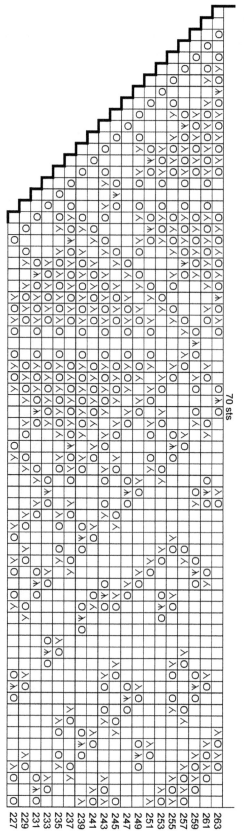

70 sts

227 229 231 233 235 237 239 241 243 245 247 249 251 253 255 257 259 261 263

(Right section of chart F continues from here.)

(Center of chart F continues from here.)

(Center of chart F continues from here.)

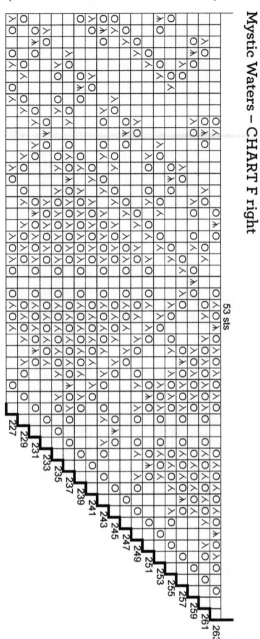

Mystic Waters – CHART F right

53 sts

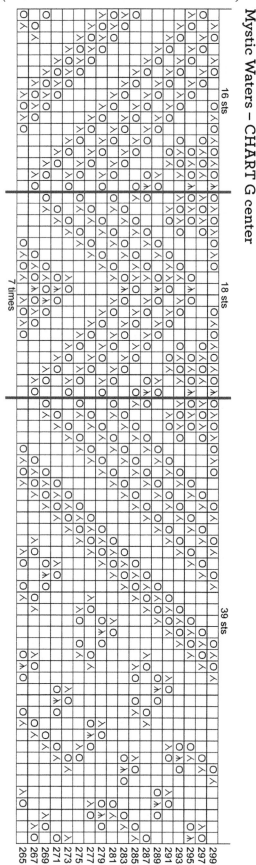

Mystic Waters – CHART G left

Mystic Waters – CHART G center

16 sts

18 sts

7 times

39 sts

73 sts

(Center of chart G continues from here.)

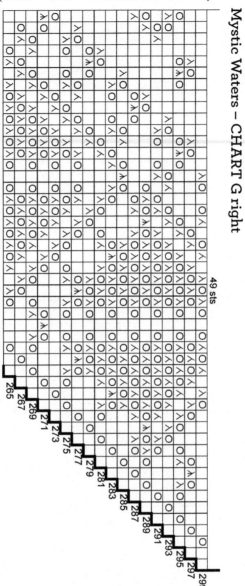

Mystic Waters – CHART G right

49 sts

265
267
269
271
273
275
277
279
281
283
285
287
289
291
293
295
297
299

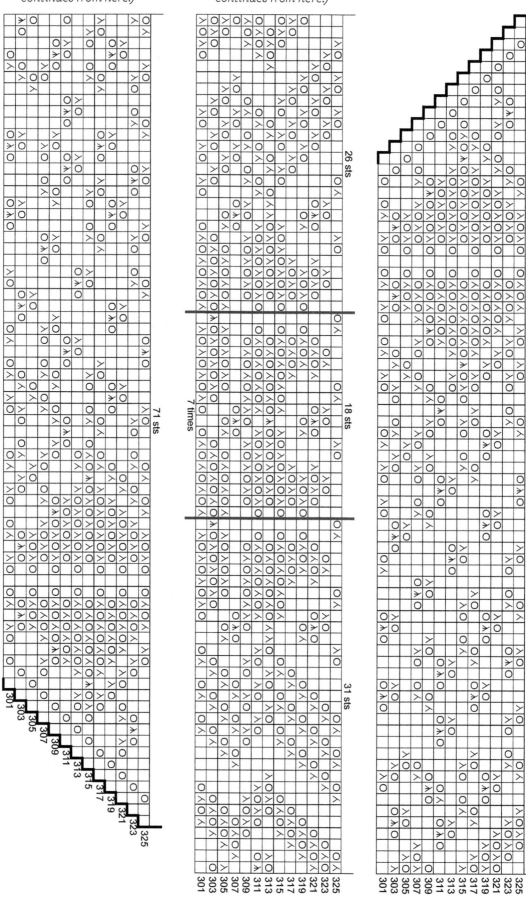

(Center of chart H
continues from here.)

(Left section of chart H
continues from here.)

26 sts

71 sts

7 times

18 sts

31 sts

75 sts

301
303
305
307
309
311
313
315
317
319
321
323
325

301 303 305 307 309 311 313 315 317 319 321 323 325

301 303 305 307 309 311 313 315 317 319 321 323 325

(Right section of chart H
continues from here.)

(Center of chart H
continues from here.)

24

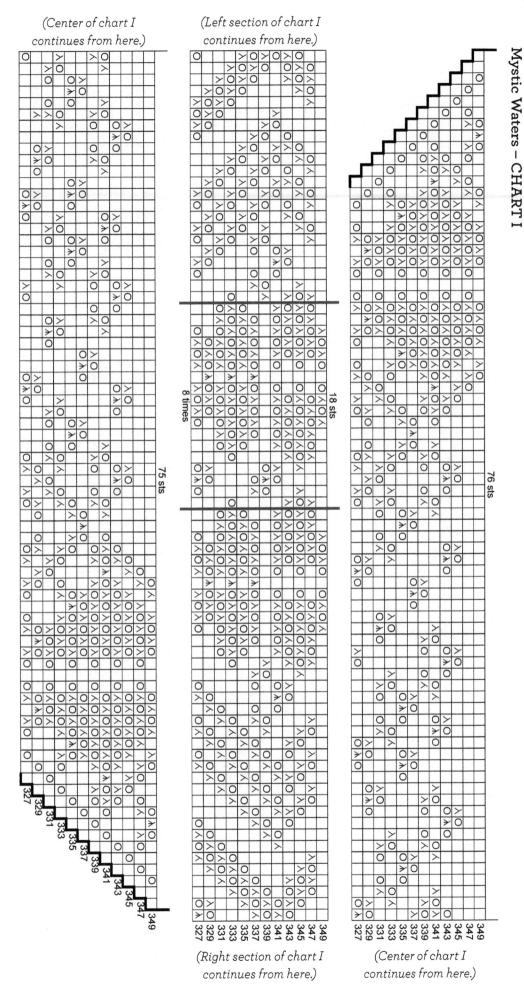

(Center of chart I
continues from here.)

(Left section of chart I
continues from here.)

8 times

18 sts

76 sts

75 sts

327
329
331
333
335
337
339
341
343
345
347
349

327
329
331
333
335
337
339
341
343
345
347
349

(Right section of chart I
continues from here.)

327
329
331
333
335
337
339
341
343
345
347
349

(Center of chart I
continues from here.)

25

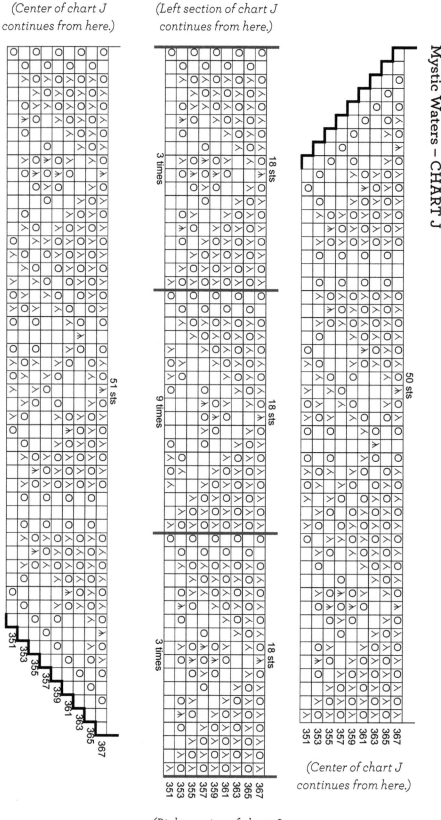

(Center of chart J
continues from here.)

(Left section of chart J
continues from here.)

(Center of chart J
continues from here.)

(Right section of chart J
continues from here.)

(Center of chart K continues from here.)

(Left section of chart K continues from here.)

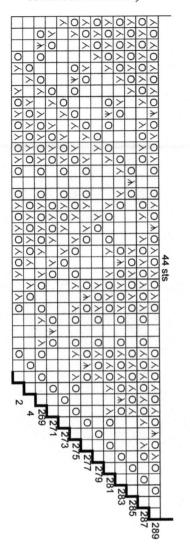

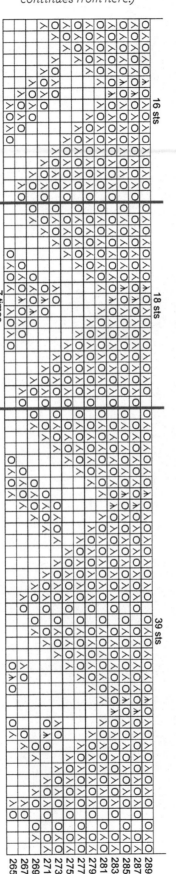

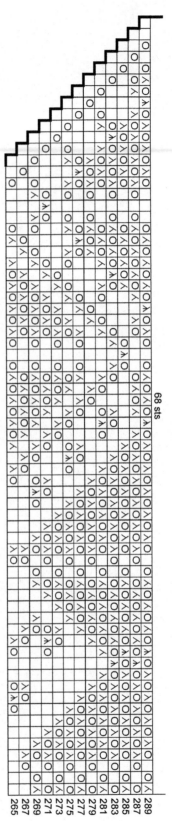

16 sts

18 sts

7 times

44 sts

39 sts

68 sts

2
4
269
271
273
275
277
279
281
283
285
287
289

265
267
269
271
273
275
277
279
281
283
285
287
289

265
267
269
271
273
275
277
279
281
283
285
287
289

(Center of chart K continues from here.)

(Right section of chart K continues from here.)

27

mystic light

This triangular shawl draws its inspiration from light in its many forms: from the silvery moonlight of a clear, starlit night to the golden, dancing flames of a warming fire.

Mystic Waters was followed by Mystic Light, a triangular shawl knit from the top-down in fingering-weight yarn. Instead of designing it with the more traditional garter stitch edging and single knit spine, I used a simple twisted cable for the edging, and a braided cable down the spine. The thicker yarn gave a nice weight to the cables. My yarn was a fiery orange.

The body of the shawl is covered by stars near the top, and a number of different types of flames—smaller ones like on candles and large, lapping flames on the lower edge.

The body of the shawl is covered by stars near the top, and a number of different types of flames.

Mystic Light

MATERIALS

2 skeins of Merino 2/6 from Fleece Artist [100% merino – 355 yds/325 m per 115 g] or similar yarn

4.5 mm [US 7] needles

Large-eyed, blunt needle

GAUGE

12.5 sts and 25 rows = 4 in [10 cm] in stockinette stitch, blocked

FINISHED (BLOCKED) SIZE

Width: 195 cm [76"], height: 97 cm [38"]

INSTRUCTIONS

CO 4 sts using a provisional cast on.

Setup row 1 (RS): K4.
Setup row 2 (WS): P4.
Setup row 3: C4F.
Setup row 4: P4.
Setup row 5: K4.
Setup row 6: P4.
Setup row 7: C4F.
Setup row 8: P4.

Setup row 9: K4, pickup and knit 8 sts along one side of the cable and 4 sts at the provisional cast on for a total of 16 sts.
Setup row 10: P16.
Setup row 11: C4F, yo, k1, yo, C4F, k2, yo, k1, yo, C4F.
Setup row 12: P20.

Then continue with the charts. Only the RS rows are charted. Rows are read from right to left.

The rows are worked as follows:

»   Row 1 (RS): K4, yo, charted row, yo, k2, C4B, yo, charted row, yo, k4.

»   Row 2 (WS): Purl.

»   Row 3: C4F, yo, charted row, yo, C4F, k2, yo, charted row, yo, C4F.

»   Row 4: Purl.

Continue in this fashion, cycling through these 4 rows until you reach row 130 of the pattern.

Work charts A–C.

Starting at row 131, both RS and WS rows are charted. Note that all RS charted rows are read from right to left. All WS charted rows are read from left to right.

The RS rows continue the cable patterns as before.

The WS rows are: P4, charted row, p6, charted row, p4.

Work charts D–E.

Continue knitting until you have completed row 172 [366 sts].

Row 173 (RS): K4, yo, k5, yo, k20, *yo, k2, p, k2, yo, k19; rep from * a total of 6 times, yo, k6, yo, k2, C4B, yo, k5, yo, k20, *yo, k2, p1, k2, yo, k19; rep from * a total of 6 times, yo, k6, yo, k4 (394 sts).

Row 174 (WS): P4, k191, p6, k191, p4.

FINISHING INSTRUCTIONS

Turn the work and BO as follows: K2, *return 2 sts to ln, k2tog through back loop, k1, rep from * until no unworked sts remain.

To get a nice edging for the cables, you should cross the cables as required (C4F for the outer edging, and C4F for the first set of 4 sts on the center cable) and then use the BO technique described above to close the sts. This means that you start the BO row by slipping the first 2 sts to cn, then slip 2 sts to rn, replace sts from cn to ln, then replace stitches from rn to ln. All sts are now back on ln, but the first cable is crossed. Then k2, *return to ln, k2tog through back loop, k1, rep from *. Continue in this fashion until you reach the center braid. There, you cross the cable and continue the BO. Again, continue until you reach the last cable (4 sts rem on the needles). Cross that cable and bind off the last few stitches.

Sew in ends and block. When blocking, pull the double tips of the flames (the yarn overs) to form points along the edging.

Christine, Leesburg, VA

Mystic Light – CHART A

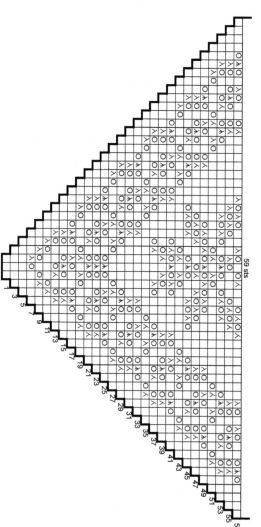

59 sts

Mystic Light – CHART C

Mystic Light – CHART B

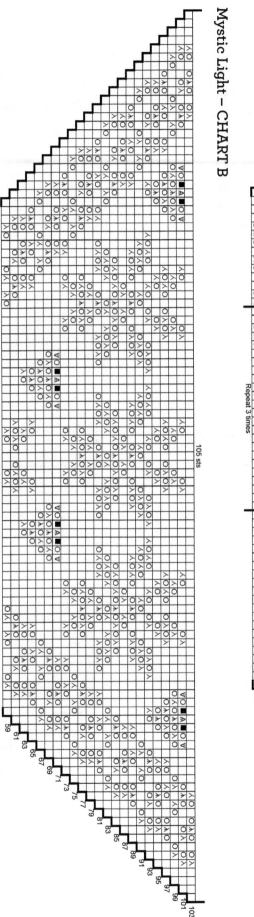
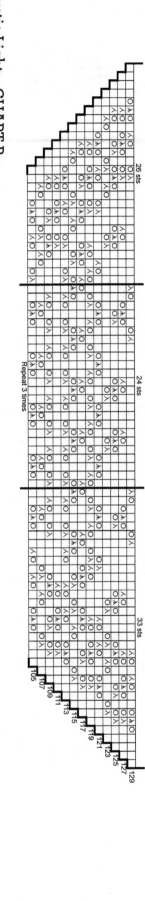

33

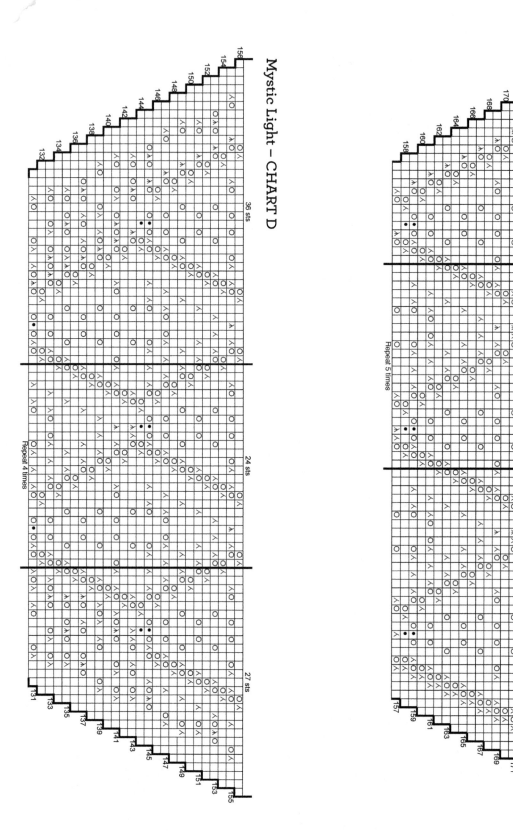

Note: Both RS and WS rows are charted above.

mystic meadows

Mystic Meadows is a rectangular stole that draws its inspiration from flowering midsummer meadows with colorful flowers of every hue.

This time, I was not experimenting with the shape of the shawl so much, but more with the types of stitches used.

The shawl starts at one edge with meandering flower stems, which are crowned with tulip-like flowers. After that, a background pattern of cables and lace is introduced, and there are some floral bouquets covering the back of the shawl. The last section is festooned with butterflies.

This shawl contains lace, cables, nupps, and various wraps. It also has lace patterning on both right side and wrong side rows to challenge the knitter. The pattern never really repeats, so there is always something new and interesting happening.

This pattern never really repeats, so there is always something new and interesting happening.

Mystic Meadows

MATERIALS

2 skeins of Signature – Superwash Sock Yarn from Brooklyn Handspun [100% merino – 480 yds/439 m per 113 g] in Prezzie or similar yarn

4.5 mm [US 7] needles

Large-eyed, blunt needle

GAUGE

13 sts and 21 rows = 4 in [10 cm] in stockinette stitch, blocked

FINISHED (BLOCKED) SIZE

Width: 75 cm [29.5"], length: 204 cm [80"]

INSTRUCTIONS

CO 95 sts with a long-tail cast on. Then continue with the charts. All rows are charted.

Options to lengthen the stole:

» Option 1: Rep rows 163–182.

» Option 2: Rep rows 273–292.

» Option 3: Rep rows 323–382.

» Option 4: After row 402, insert a rep of 163–182 to add some length at the end.

FINISHING INSTRUCTIONS

Bind off as follows: K2, *return 2 sts to ln, k2tog through back loop, k1, rep from * until no unworked sts remain.

Sew in ends and block.

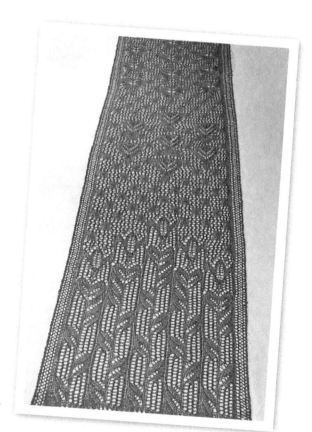

Rita Miller, Gonzales, LA

Mystic Meadows – CHART A

8 sts · 16 sts · 7 sts

5 times

95 sts

Mystic Meadows – CHART C

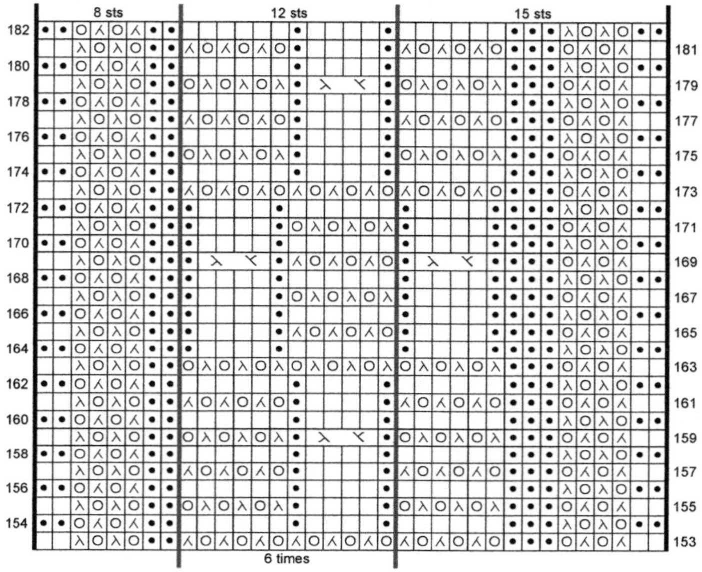
8 sts
12 sts
15 sts
182
180
178
176
174
172
170
168
166
164
162
160
158
156
154
181
179
177
175
173
171
169
167
165
163
161
159
157
155
153
6 times

95 sts

43

Mystic Meadows – CHART E

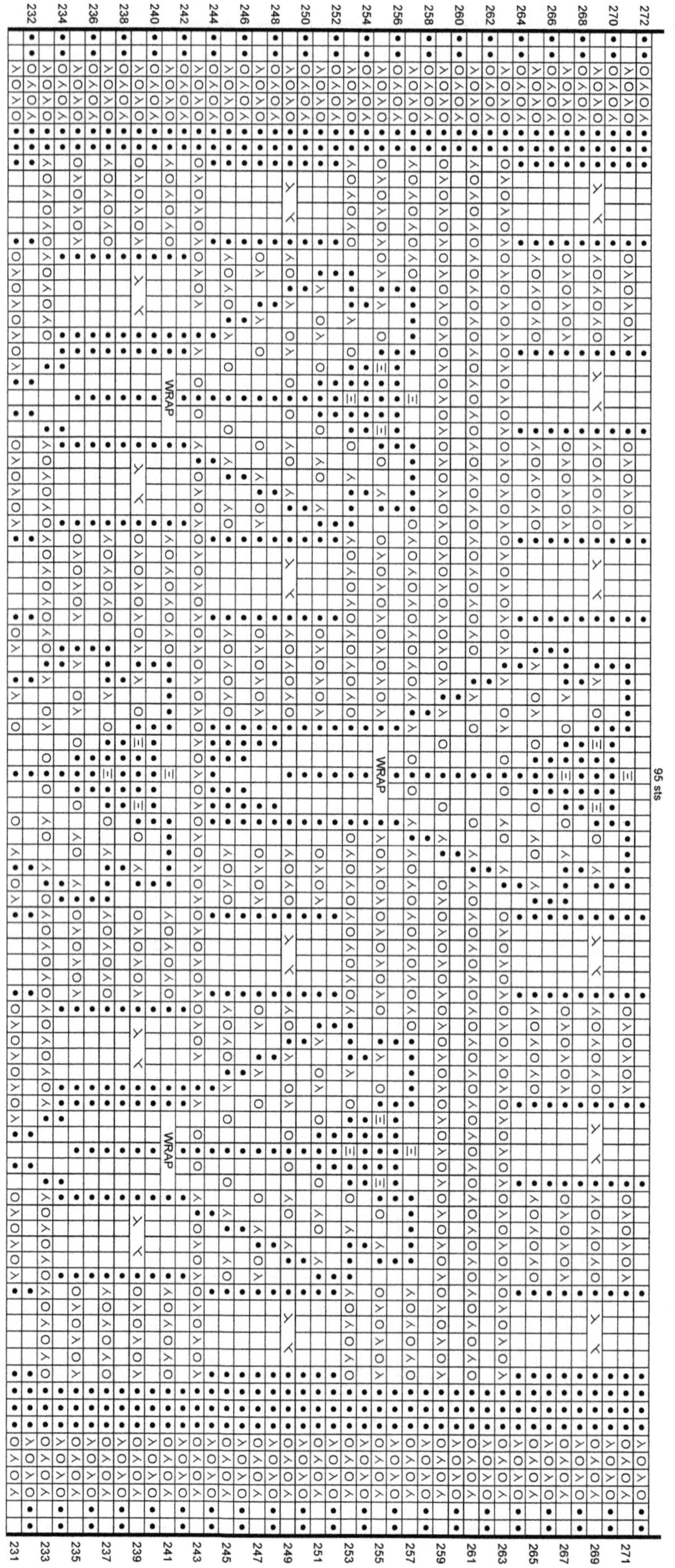

Mystic Meadows – CHART F

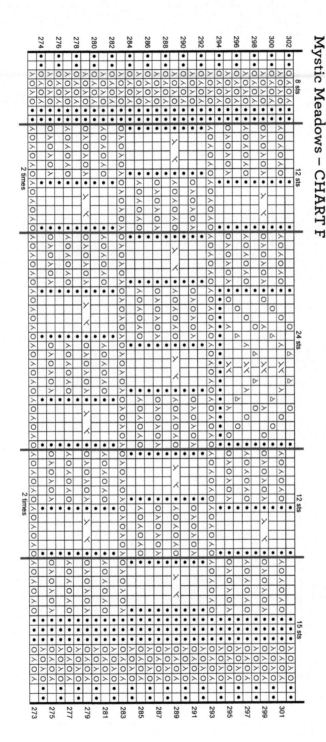

45

Mystic Meadows – CHART G

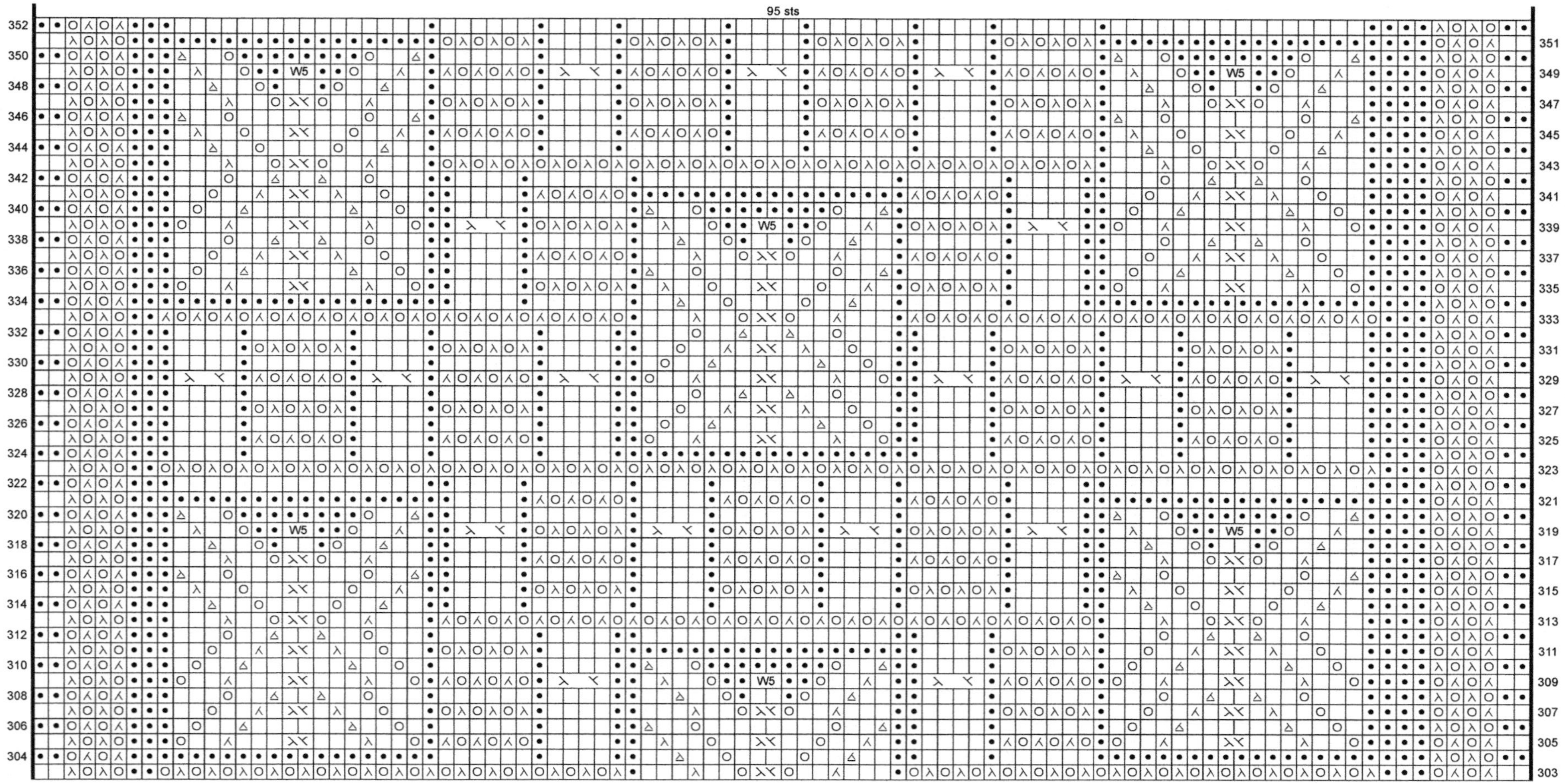

Mystic Meadows – CHART H

Mystic Meadows – CHART I

47

mystic earth

This rectangular stole was the third shawl chronologically in the Mystic Elements series (following Mystic Waters and Mystic Light). Mystic Earth draws its inspiration from the solid earth beneath our feet: its constant presence and its ever-changing seasons.

The construction of this shawl was inspired by Russian lace. There are no outside cast-on or bound-off stitches. The shawl starts with a provisional cast on and the bottom border. The stitches are then picked up along the inside edge of the border for the body of the stole. The left- and right-side edgings are knit along with the shawl. Finally, the top border is knit across the top, and the last few stitches are grafted to the top of the left edging.

Unlike most Russian lace though, the Mystic Earth stole is stockinette-based lace.

This stole has four sections, representing the four seasons. It starts with delicate spring leaves. In the second section, intricate flowers signal the arrival of summer. For autumn, there are bundles of hay, and in the winter, a stark frost pattern spreads over the windowpanes.

The shawl was knit using Buffalo Down yarn from Cottage Craft Angora. It is a heavier laceweight with a soft halo to it. After blocking, the halo spreads slightly, and when held up against the light you can see the fibers in the lacy holes. This results in a very warm fabric with a delicate but still earthy look.

This stole has four sections representing the four seasons—spring, summer, fall and winter.

Mystic Earth

MATERIALS

7 skeins of Luxurious Buffalo Down from Cottage Craft Angora [100% buffalo down – 155 yds/142 m per 22 g] or similar yarn for the stole (3 skeins needed for scarf version)

3.75 mm [US 5] needles

Large-eyed, blunt needle

GAUGE

21 sts and 40 rows = 4 in [10 cm] in stockinette stitch, blocked

FINISHED (BLOCKED) SIZE

Stole: width: 65 cm [25.5"], length: 201 cm [79"]

Scarf: width: 32 cm [12.5"], length: 201 cm [79"]

STOLE INSTRUCTIONS

CO 12 sts with a provisional cast on.

Work rows 1–20 of the bottom border chart 9 times, then work rows 21–22 once.

Bottom Border

Place a marker. Pick up and purl 90 sts (one in each bump along the edge) plus 1 stitch at the end. Place marker. Purl the first 9 sts from the provisional cast on, and knit the last 2 sts from the provisional cast on.

At this point, you should have 113 sts on your needles (11+91+11).

Main Body

Start working on the main body of the shawl using charts A–I.

Top Border

With the RS of the stole facing you, knit rows 1–20 of the top border 9 times.

(The k2tog at the end of each RS rows knits the border together with a stitch on the main body.)

When you have worked the top border 9 times, 1 stitch remains on the main body of the shawl. Work row 1 of the top border, joining it with the last stitch on the main body, and graft the top border to the left border.

Sew in ends and block.

Rita Miller, Gonzales, LA

SCARF INSTRUCTIONS

CO 12 sts with a provisional cast on.

Work rows 1–20 of the bottom border chart 3 times, then work rows 21–22 once.

Bottom Border

Place a marker. Pick up and purl 30 sts (one in each bump along the edge) plus 1 stitch at the end. Place marker. Purl the first 9 sts from the provisional cast on, and knit the last 2 sts from the provisional cast on.

At this point, you should have 53 sts on your needles (11+31+11).

Main Body

Start working on the main body of the shawl using scarf charts A–F (which begin on 62).

Top Border

With the RS of the scarf facing you, knit rows 1–20 of the top border 3 times.

(The k2tog at the end of each RS rows knits the border together with a stitch on the main body.)

When you have worked the top border 3 times, 1 stitch remains on the main body of the scarf. Work row 1 of the top border, joining it with the last stitch on the main body, and graft the top border to the left border.

Sew in ends and block.

Mystic Earth – BOTTOM BORDER CHART

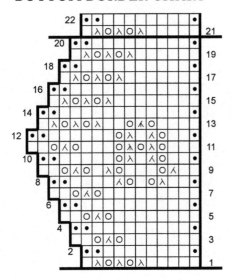

Mystic Earth – TOP BORDER CHART

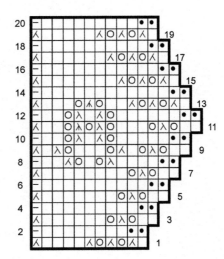

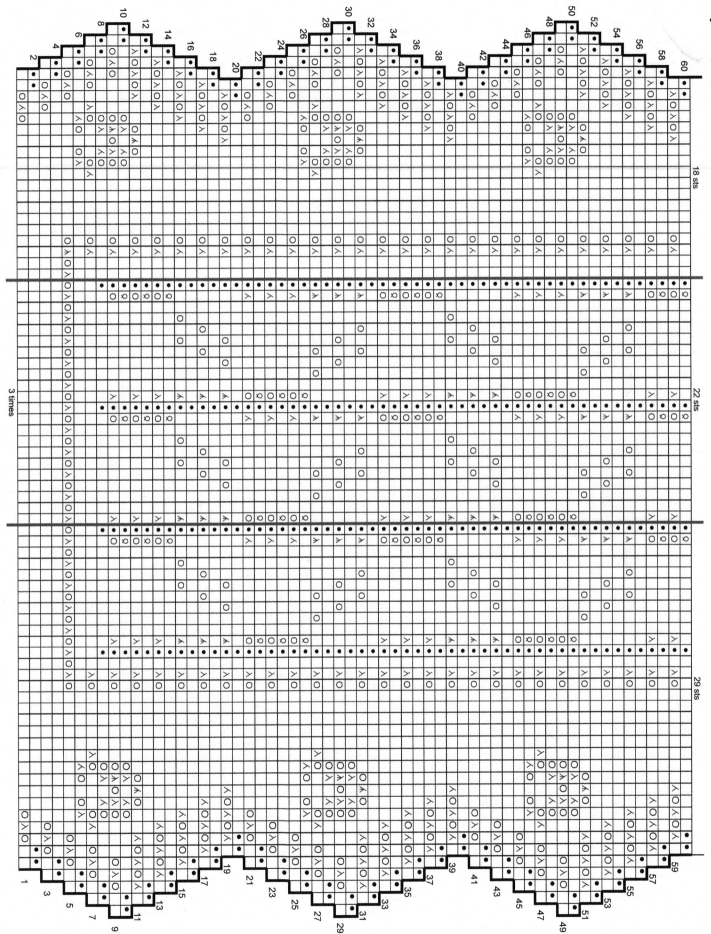

Mystic Earth Shawl – CHART A

18 sts

22 sts

3 times

29 sts

53

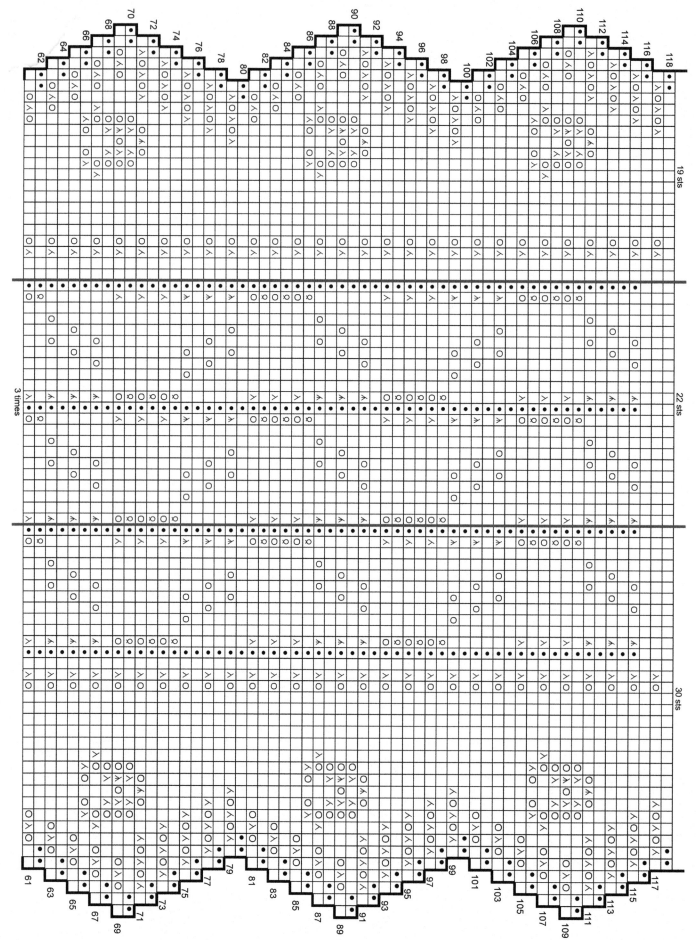

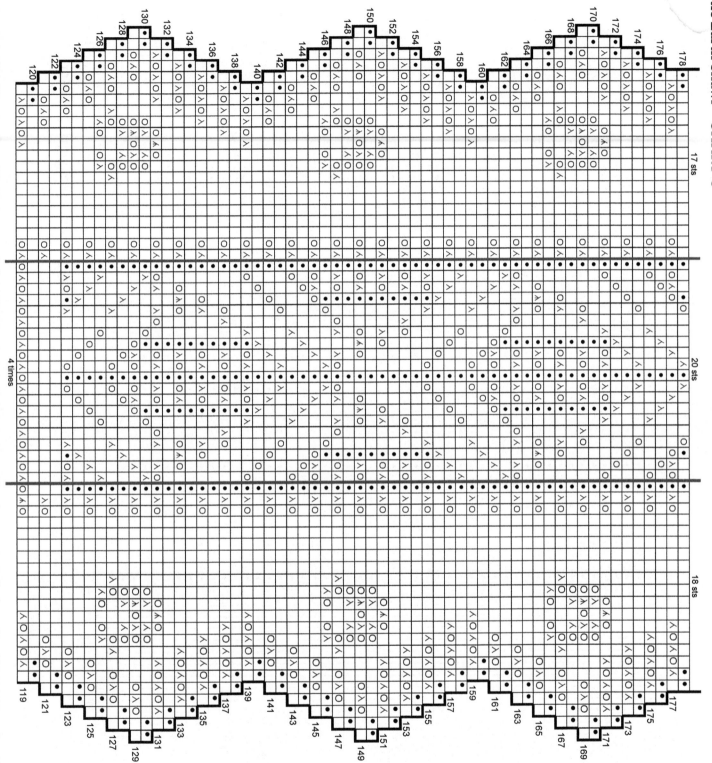

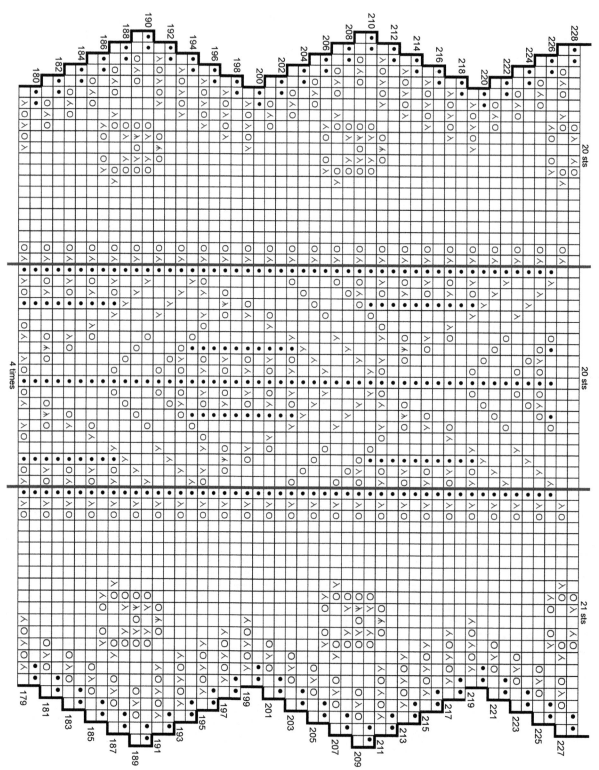

56

Mystic Earth Shawl – CHART E

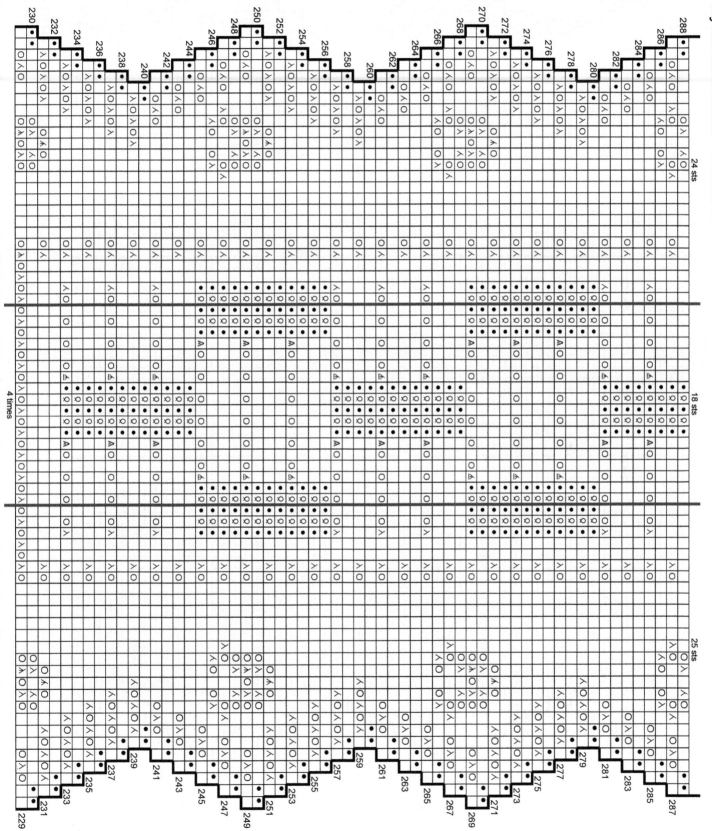

57

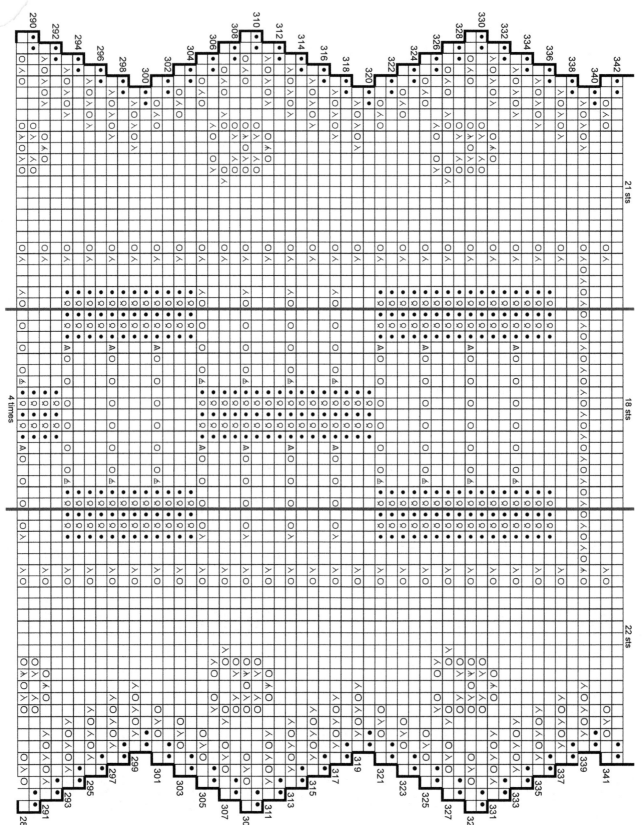

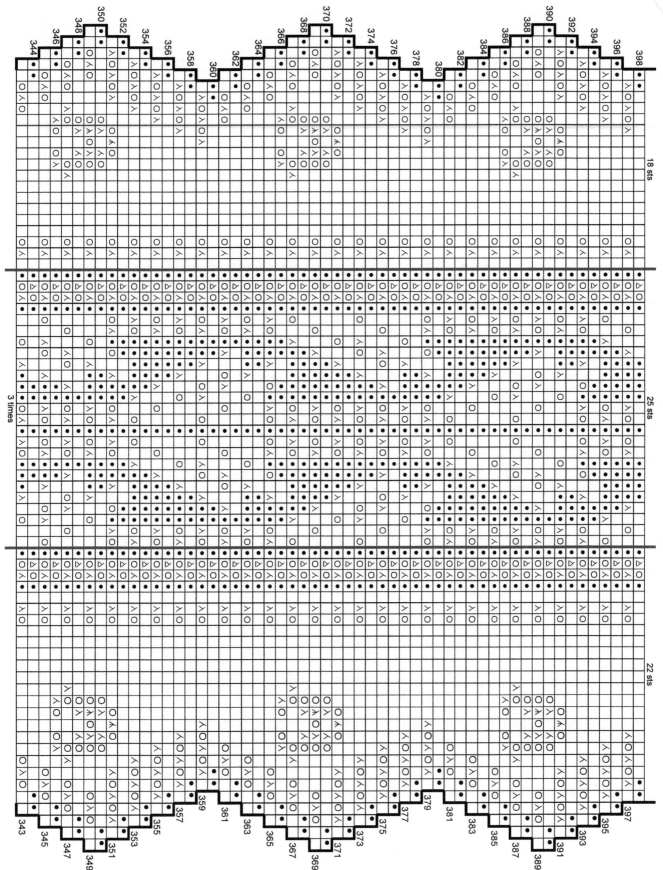

Mystic Earth Shawl – CHART H

60

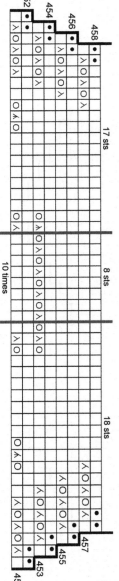

Mystic Earth Shawl – CHART I

Mystic Earth Scarf – CHART A

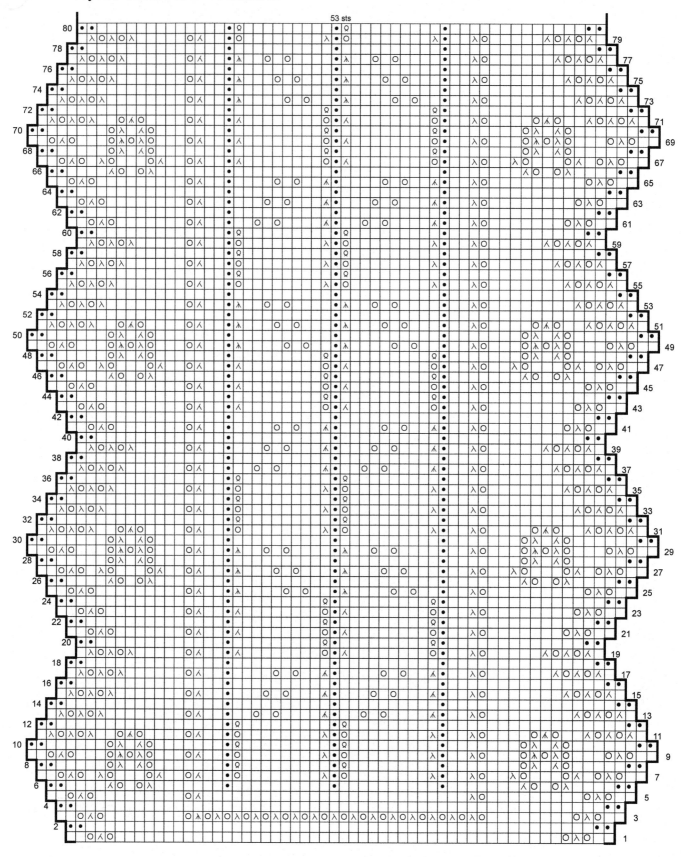

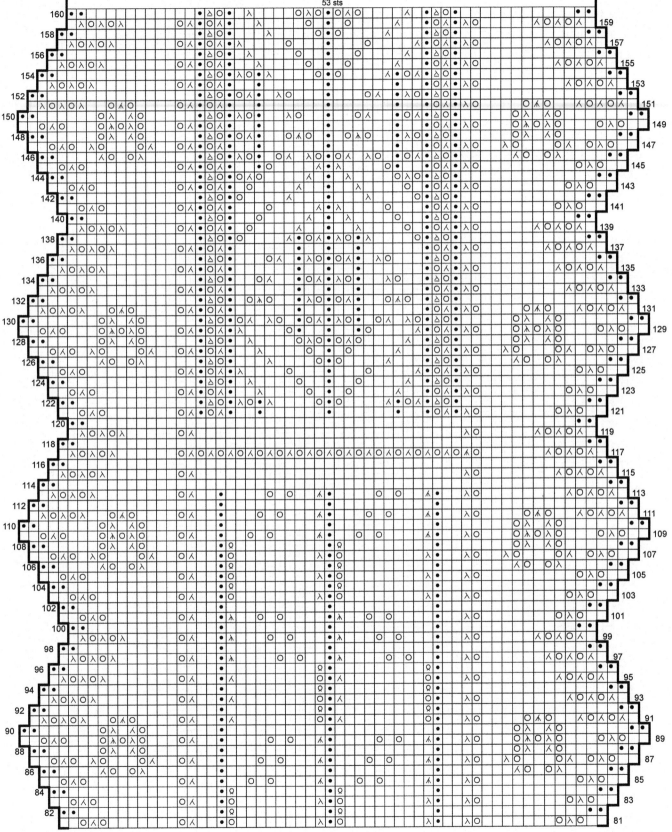

Mystic Earth Scarf – CHART C

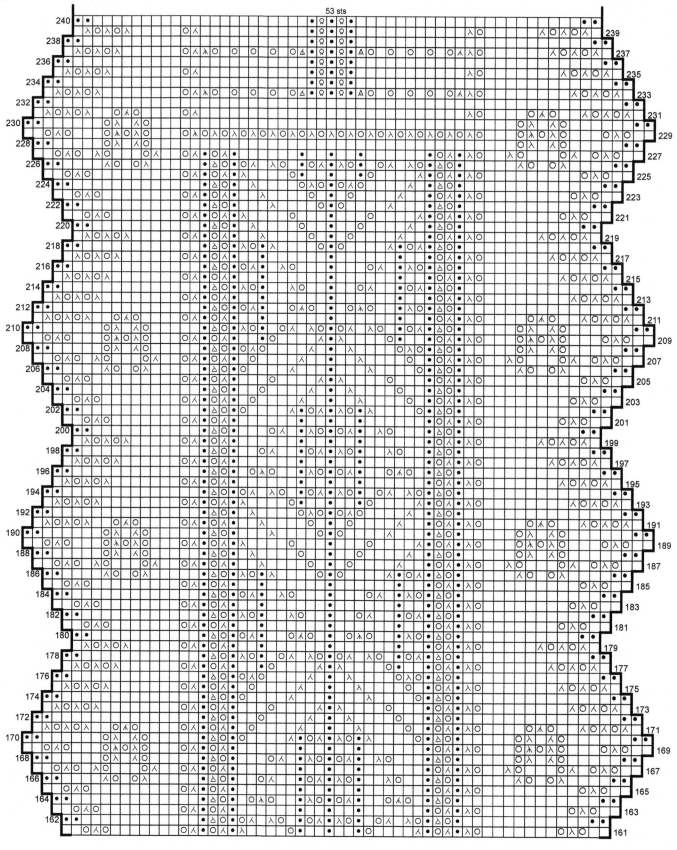

64

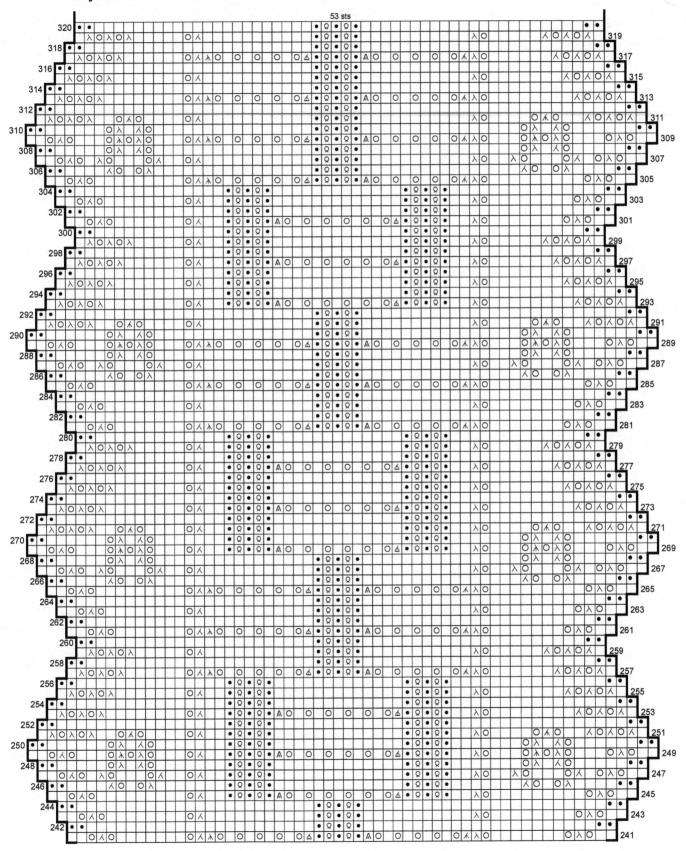

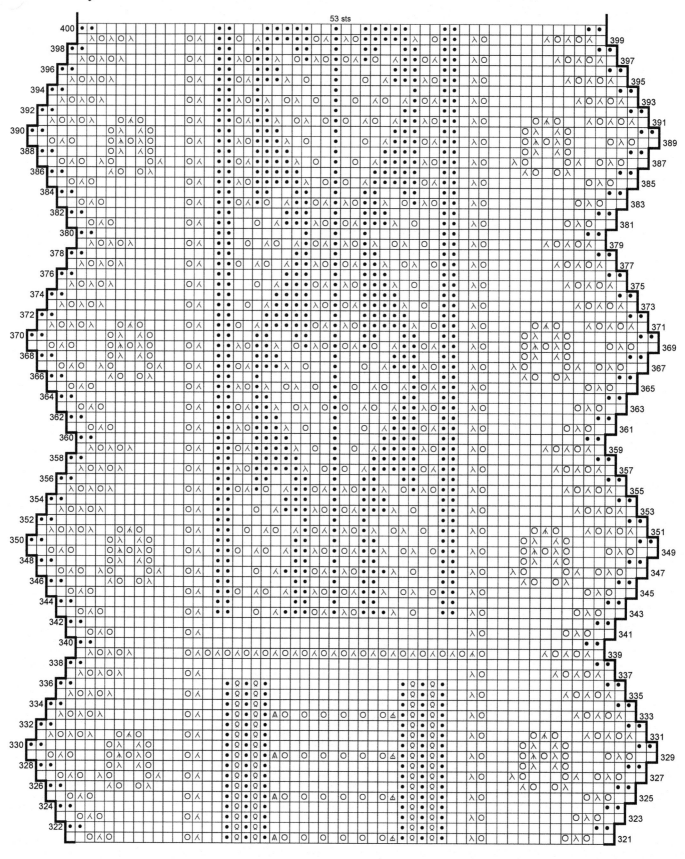

Mystic Earth Scarf – CHART F

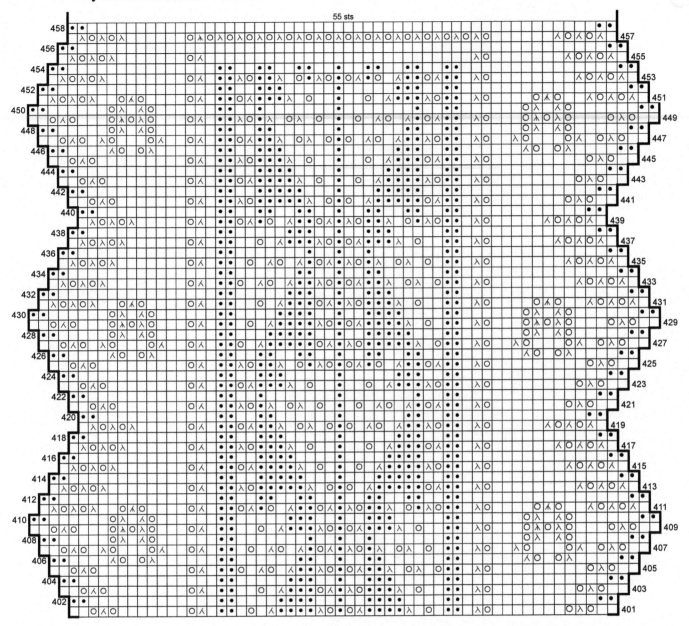

55 sts

mystic ice

This shawl draws its inspiration from winter, and in particular the breathtaking icicles found during the early and late parts of the season.

The shawl is available in either a square or triangular shape (or why not knit one of each?).

In this pattern, I wanted to translate Celtic cables into lace patterning. Each strand of the imaginary cable was translated into three yarn-overs with matching decreases. There is a definite direction in which the cables "cross" each other in the lace pattern.

The shawl was knit using lace-weight Tencel yarn from Yarntopia Treasures. This was the first time I had ever worked with Tencel, or even heard of the fiber. It is often referred to as "poor man's silk," and it does indeed share many characteristics with silk. Tencel is shiny, very strong and creates a fabric with gorgeous drape. It accepts dyes readily and can be dyed in anything from rich jewel tones to pastels.

The price of Tencel, however, is only a fraction of the price of silk. It's a cellulose fiber made from wood pulp, and is often touted as an environmentally friendly alternative, in the same category as other manmade fibers like soy silk, milk fiber, and Seacell. That said, some sources claim that while the wood pulp itself is environmentally friendly and natural, the processing used in creating the fiber includes a number of chemicals, so it is unclear how environmentally friendly it is.

All in all, used in lace knitting, Tencel results in a shiny, luxurious feeling shawl with amazing drape.

Rita Miller, Gonzales, LA

Mystic Ice

MATERIALS

2 skeins of Lace Yarn from Yarntopia Treasures [100% Tencel – 1000 yds/ 960 m per 115 g] in Seaweed or similar yarn for square shawl (1 skein for triangular shawl)

3.25 mm [US 3] circular needle

3.25 mm [US 3] DPNs

Cable needle

Stitch markers

Large-eyed, blunt needle

GAUGE

12 sts and 24 rows = 4 in [10 cm] in pattern, blocked

FINISHED (BLOCKED) SIZE

Square: 150 cm [59"] square

Triangle: wingspan: 175 cm [70"], height: 87 cm [35"]

SQUARE SHAWL INSTRUCTIONS

CO 8 sts using invisible loop (see http://techknitting.blogspot.com/2007/02/casting-on-from-middle-disappearing.html for tutorial).

Divide evenly on 4 DPNs (switch to circular needle when you have enough stitches on the needles, or use magic loop).

Setup rnd 1: K8, place a marker to mark the beginning of the rnds.
Setup rnd 2: [C2B, yo] 4 times.
Setup rnd 3: K12.

Work charts A–D as follows:

» Odd rnds: [C2B, yo, charted row, yo] 4 times.

» Even rnds: Knit.

FINISHING INSTRUCTIONS

Rnd 240: Purl.

Bind off as follows: K2, *return to ln, k2tog through back loop, k1, rep from * until no unworked sts remain.

Sew in ends and block. When blocking, pull each of the peaks to a point for the edging.

TRIANGULAR SHAWL INSTRUCTIONS

CO 6 sts using long-tail cast on.

Setup row 1: P6.
Setup row 2: C2B, yo, C2B, yo, C2B.
Setup row 3: P8.

Work charts A–D as follows:

» RS rows: C2B, yo, charted row, yo, C2B, yo, charted row, yo, C2B.

» WS rows: Purl.

FINISHING INSTRUCTIONS

Row 240: Knit.

Bind off as follows: K2, *return to ln, k2tog through back loop, k1, rep from * until no unworked sts remain.

Sew in ends and block. When blocking, pull each of the peaks to a point for the edging.

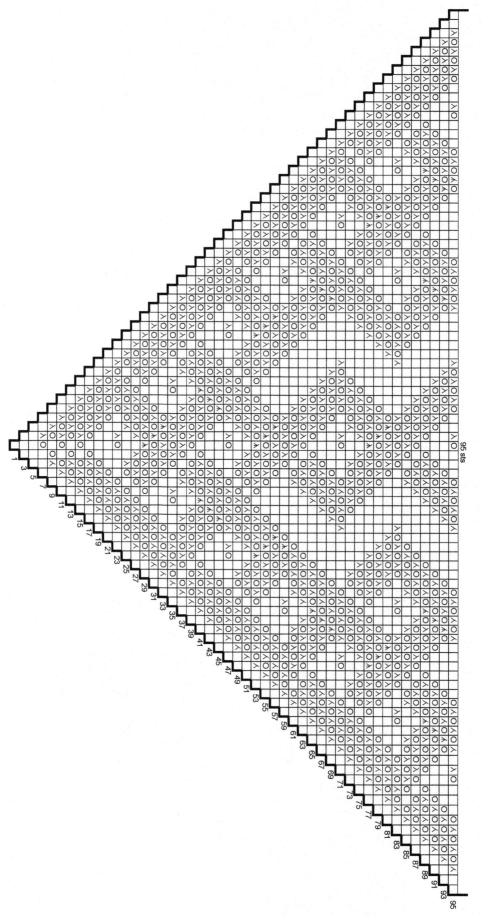

95 sts

(Left half of chart B continues from here.)

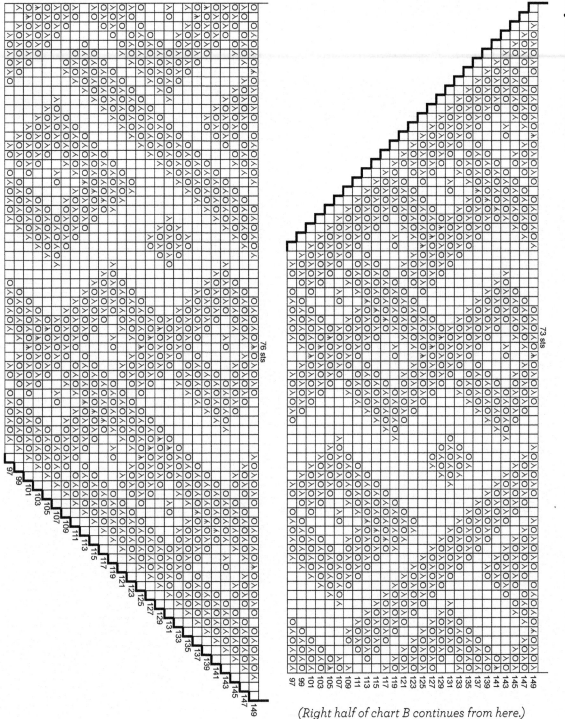

76 sts

73 sts

(Right half of chart B continues from here.)

73

(Left half of chart C continues from here.)

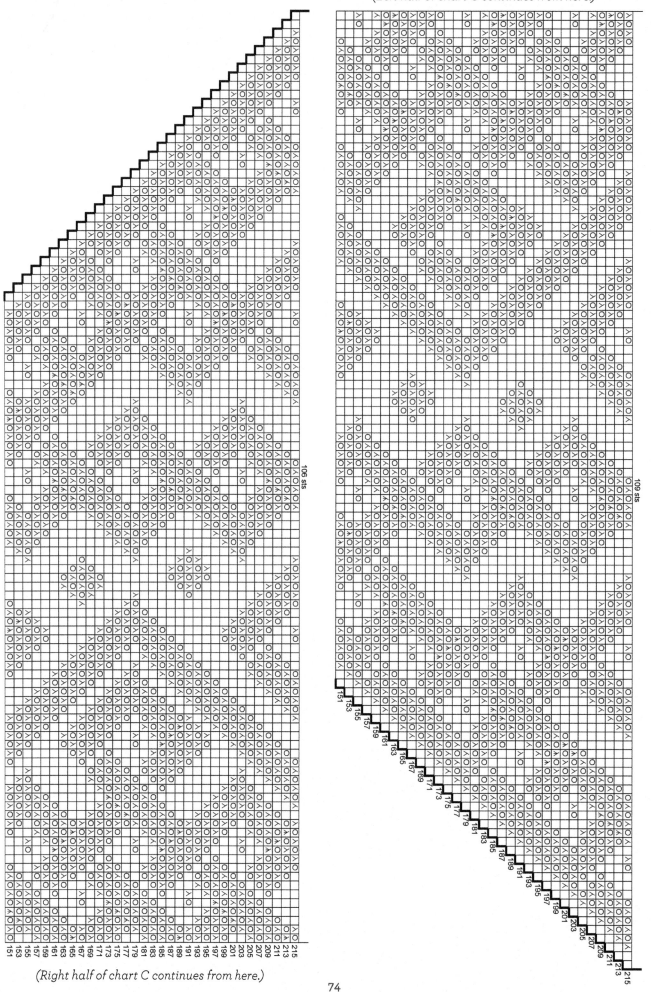

109 sts

106 sts

(Right half of chart C continues from here.)

(Left half of chart D continues from here.)

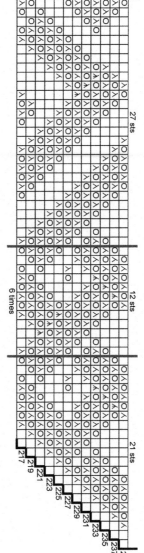

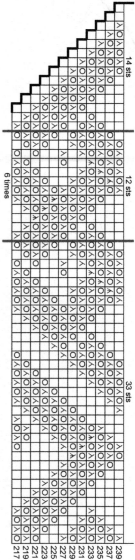

(Right half of chart D continues from here.)

75

mystic star

This circular shawl draws its inspiration from the starry night sky.

After Mystic Ice, which was a square shawl knit in the round, I wanted to try creating a circular shawl using Elizabeth Zimmermann's pi shawl construction. Pi shawls rely on the relationship between the circumference of the shawl (the number of stitches) and the radius of the shawl (the number of rounds, counting out from the center). Basically, each time the radius doubles, the circumference doubles. And since knit fabric is stretchy by nature, it's sufficient to double the number of stitches every time the radius doubles. The stitches are increased in special increase rounds which are worked in repeats of [k1, yo] to the end.

When knitting in the round, repeating a fairly simple pattern of diamonds will result in a spectacular-looking star motif. This shawl uses both lace patterning and "negative space"—that is, the plain stockinette separating the lace motifs—to create the stars.

In the outermost section of the shawl, I have translated Nordic stars (popular in Fair Isle knits) into lace patterns. A wave pattern completes the shawl.

Like Mystic Ice, this shawl is also knit in Tencel. (See page 81 for a description of Tencel yarn.)

Mystic Star can be knit as a circle or a semi-circle.

Semi-circular shawl
Rita Miller, Gonzales, LA

Mystic Star

MATERIALS

1 skein of Lace Yarn from Yarntopia Treasures [100% tencel – 1000 yds/ 960 m per 115 g] in Seaweed or similar yarn for circular shawl (0.5 skeins for semi-circular shawl)

3.25 mm [US 3] circular needle

3.25 mm [US 3] DPNs

Stitch markers

Large-eyed, blunt needle

GAUGE

12 sts and 24 rows = 4 in [10 cm] in pattern, blocked

FINISHED (BLOCKED) SIZE

Diameter: 130 cm [51"]

CIRCULAR SHAWL INSTRUCTIONS

CO 9 sts using the invisible loop technique. (For a tutorial, see techknitting.blogspot.com/2007/02/ casting-on-from-middle-disappearing. html).

Divide sts evenly on 3 DPNs. (Switch to circular needle when you have enough sts on the needles, or use magic loop.)

Rnd 1: K9, place a marker to mark the beginning of the rows.

Rnd 2: [K1, yo] 9 times (18 sts). Rnds 3–5: Knit.

Rnd 6: [K1, yo] 18 times (36 sts). Rnds 7–12: Knit.

Rnd 13: [K1, yo] 36 times (72 sts).

Note: All even-numbered rnds from this point are knit.

Section 1

Work Chart A 12 times around.

Rnd 27: [K1, yo] 72 times (144 sts). Rnd 28: Knit.

Section 2

Work Chart B 12 times around.

Rnd 53: [K1, yo] 144 times (288 sts). Rnd 54: Knit.

Section 3

Work Chart C 12 times around.

Rnd 103: [K1, yo] 288 times (576 sts). Rnd 104: Knit.

Section 4

Work Chart D 12 times around.

FINISHING INSTRUCTIONS

Knit one plain rnd after rnd 177, then bind off as follows: K2, *return to ln, k2tog through back loop, k1, rep from * until no unworked sts remain.

Sew in ends and block. When blocking, pull each of the 24 peaks of the wave pattern to a point for the edging.

SEMI-CIRCULAR SHAWL INSTRUCTIONS

1 skein of Lace Yarn from Yarntopia Treasures [100% tencel – 1,000 yds/960 m per 115 g] in Seaweed or similar yarn (0.5 skeins for semi-circular shawl)

3.25 mm [US 3] circular needle

3.25 mm [US 3] DPNs

Stitch markers

Large-eyed, blunt needle

INSTRUCTIONS

CO 2 sts using the knitted cast on.

Setup row 1: Kfb twice (4 sts).
Setup row 2: Kfb 4 times (8 sts).
Setup row 3: K2, p4, k2.

All WS rows (even-numbered rows) are K2, purl to last 2 sts, k2.

Row 1: K2, [yo, k1] 4 times, yo, k2 (13 sts).

Row 3: K13.

Row 5: K2, [k1, yo] 9 times, k2 (22 sts).

Rows 7, 9, and 11: K22.

Row 13: K2, [k1,yo] 18 times, k2 (40 sts).

Note: All even-numbered rows from this point are K2, purl to the last 2 sts, k2.

Section 1

RS rows: K2, [chart A] 6 times, k2.

Row 27: K2, [k1, yo] 36 times, k2 (76 sts).
Row 28: K2, p72, k2.

Section 2

RS rows: K2, [chart B] 6 times, k2.

Row 53: K2, [k1, yo] 72 times, k2 (148 sts).
Row 54: K2, p144, k2.

Section 3

RS rows: K2, [chart C] 6 times, k2.

Notes:

» For row 75, the symbol in blue needs to be replaced with a k2tog in the first rep.

» And at the end of the row, instead of finishing with k2 as usual, finish with ssk, k1.

Row 103: K2, [k1, yo] 144 times, k2 (292 sts).
Row 104: K2, p288, k2.

Section 4

RS rows: K2, [chart D] 6 times, k2.

FINISHING INSTRUCTIONS

Row 178: K2, purl to last 2 sts, k2.

Turn the work and bind off as follows: k2, *return to ln, k2tog through back loop, k1, rep from * until no unworked sts remain.

Sew in ends and block. When blocking, pull each of the 12 peaks of the wave pattern to a point for the edging.

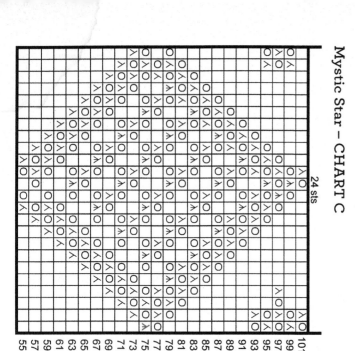

Mystic Star – CHART A

6 sts

15 17 19 21 23 25

Mystic Star – CHART B

12 sts

29 31 33 35 37 39 41 43 45 47 49 51

Mystic Star – CHART C

24 sts

55 57 59 61 63 65 67 69 71 73 75 77 79 81 83 85 87 89 91 93 95 97 99 101

Mystic Star – CHART D

48 sts

105 107 109 111 113 115 117 119 121 123 125 127 129 131 133 135 137 139 141 143 145 147 149 151 153 155 157 159 161 163 165 167 169 171 173 175 177

mystic roses

Mystic Roses is a triangular shawl inspired by roses of every hue.

Actually, Mystic Roses came about because I was hoping to try some of the mythical Wollmeise yarn that the online world was abuzz about at the time. Purchasing the yarn was a feat in and of itself. Unlike most yarn, which you can purchase by visiting the dyer's website, Wollmeise was so popular that it would sell out in minutes. And the demand was so high that taking preorders was not an option. Instead, the yarn would be made available at random times, and if you were lucky you might visit the site in the minute or so before it sold out.

I tried for weeks to get my hands on some of this yarn, and eventually I did manage to purchase one skein of laceweight. I didn't really have any choice in colors—but as it turned out, the one that was available at the time was lovely. It was called Rosenrot (rose red), and the name of the color was the seed that grew into this design.

I was trying to play with construction, and I thought that it would be fun to design a top-down triangular shawl, but instead of only using the triangles as the canvas for my design, I wanted to also add some interesting patterns on the border and down the spine. So instead of using a plain garter stitch edge across the top, I added a wide lace panel with stylized rose stems and leaves. The same panel would work down the shawl's center spine. I covered the main body with little rosebuds fashioned out of lace and cables, and then on the bottom border I knit the roses themselves, attached to the stems.

I was trying to use up most of the yarn, but Wollmeise Lace-Garn comes in very generously sized skeins of 300g and almost 1,600m. And since there is a limit to the size of the shawl one can reasonably wear, I decided to wrap the design up at a height of 134 cm and a wingspan of 268 cm. I also added a smaller size to the pattern, for people who wanted a more modest size. For me though, the large size of the shawl makes it one of my favorites.

Unlike most yarn, which you can purchase by visiting the dyer's website, Wollmeise was so popular that it would sell out in minutes.

Mystic Roses

MATERIALS

1 skein of Wollmeise Lace-Garn [100% wool; 1740 yds /1590 m per 300 g] in Rosenrot or similar yarn

3.75 mm (US 5) needles

Cable needle

Large-eyed, blunt needle

FINISHED (BLOCKED) SIZE

height (large size): 134 cm (52"), wingspan 268 cm (105")

The triangular diagram at the bottom of this page illustrates the layout of the shawl, as worn.

After the setup instructions, you will have 3 triangles on your needles, as shown in the diagram at top right.

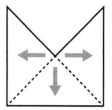

SETUP

CO 9 sts using a cabled cast on.

Setup row 1 (RS): K9.
Setup row 2 (WS): K2, p5, k2.

The next 22 rows are knit as follows:

» RS rows: K2, work setup chart, k1, setup chart, k1, setup chart, k2.

» WS rows: K2, purl to the last 2 sts, k2.

SETUP CHART

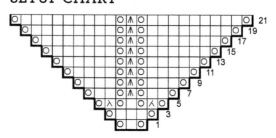

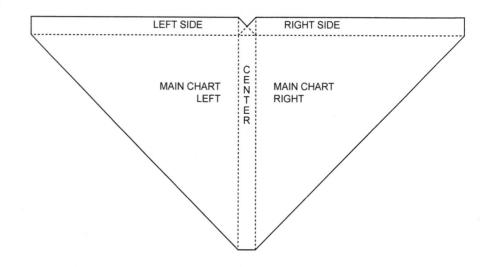

The rest of the shawl will be worked as follows:

» RS rows: K2, left side, ChartXleft, center, ChartXright, right side, k2.

» WS rows: K2, purl to the last 2 sts, k2.

The left-side, center and right-side charts (shown at right) consist of 20 rows that will be repeated as the shawl grows.

You will note that the three charts are very similar. The difference lies in the decreases in the two first and two last columns of your chart.

For reference, the main chart will include a chart with the main part of the side and center patterns. I found this very useful when lining up the side and center patterns to the main chart. However, this reference chart will include all the decreases. You must remember that they are actually knit differently depending on which chart you should be using.

LEFT-SIDE

CENTER

RIGHT-SIDE

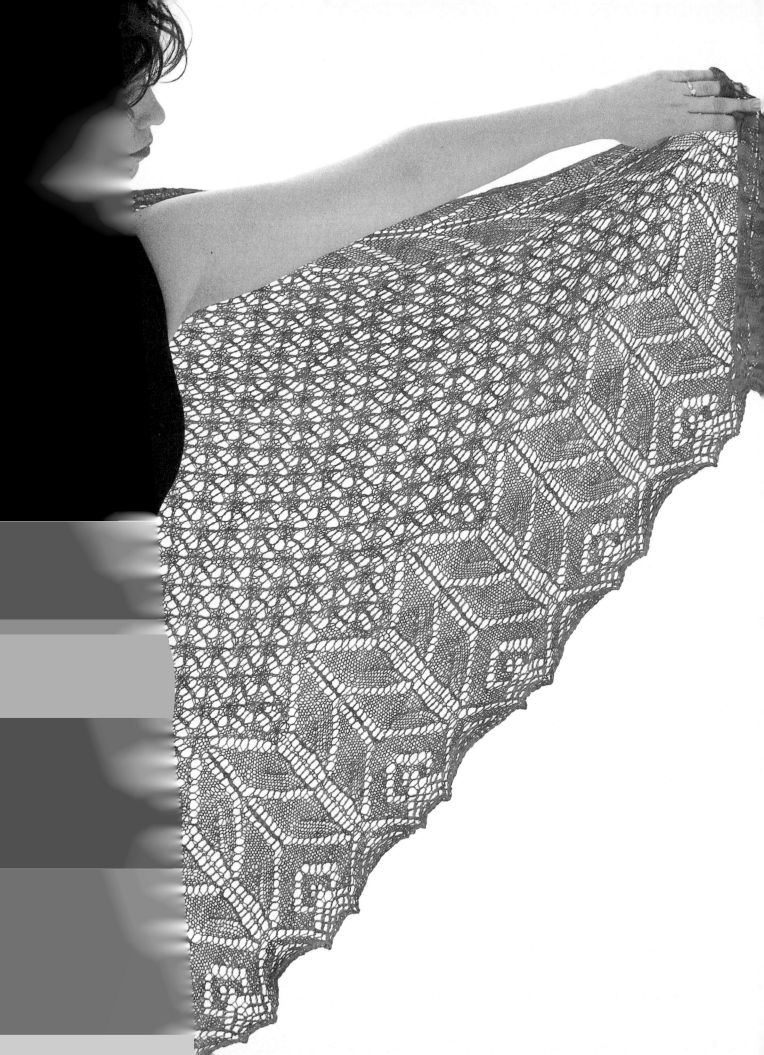

LARGE VERSION OF MYSTIC ROSES

Work the body of the shawl using charts A–D. Then work chart E. Note that for chart E, the left, center and right-side charts are included, and should be worked as written.

Row 234: K2, purl to the last 2 sts, k2.

Proceed to the finishing instructions.

SMALL VERSION OF MYSTIC ROSES

Work the body of the shawl using charts A–C, but stop at row 112. After row 112, work charts F–G.

Note that for Chart G, the left, center and right-side charts are included, and should be worked as written.

Row 194: K2, purl to the last 2 sts, k2.

Proceed to the finishing instructions.

FINISHING INSTRUCTIONS

Turn the work and bind off as follows: k2, *return sts to ln, k2tog through back loop, k1, rep from * until no unworked sts remain.

Sew in ends and block. When blocking, pull each of the shaded yarn overs on the last row of the chart to a point for the edging.

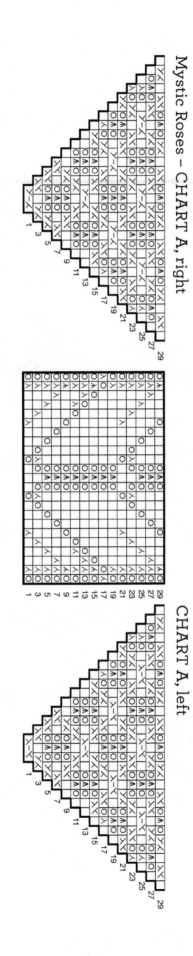

Mystic Roses – CHART A, right

CHART A, left

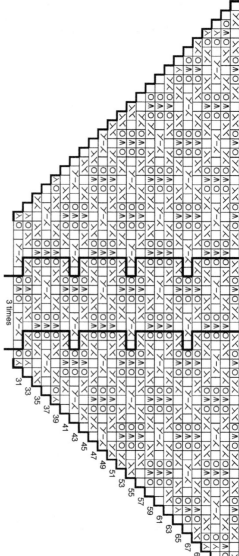

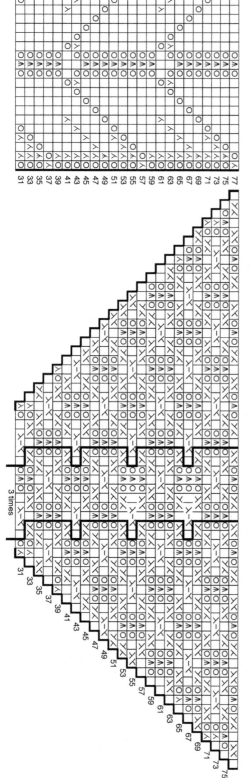

CHART B, left

90

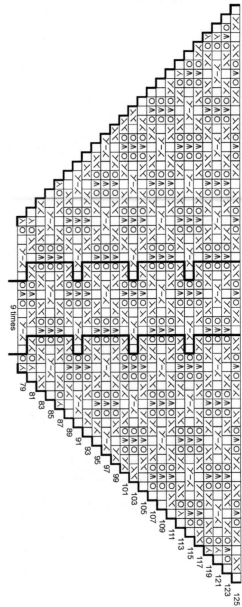

9 times

CHART C, left

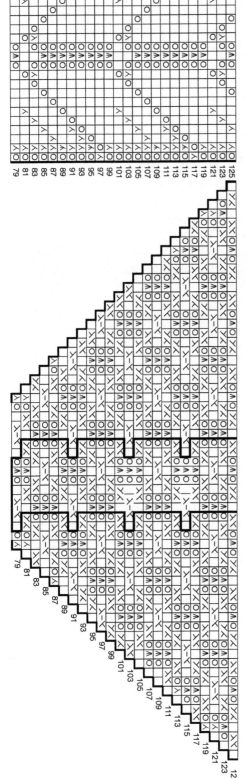

91

Mystic Roses – CHART D, right

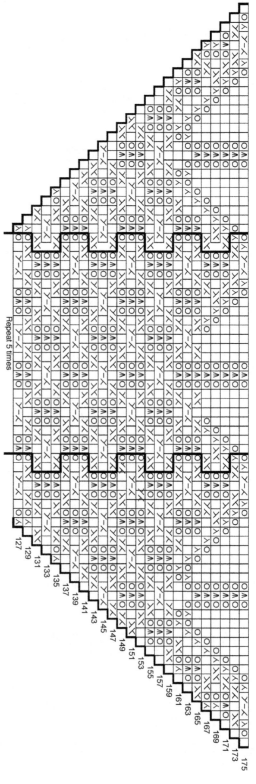

CHART D, left

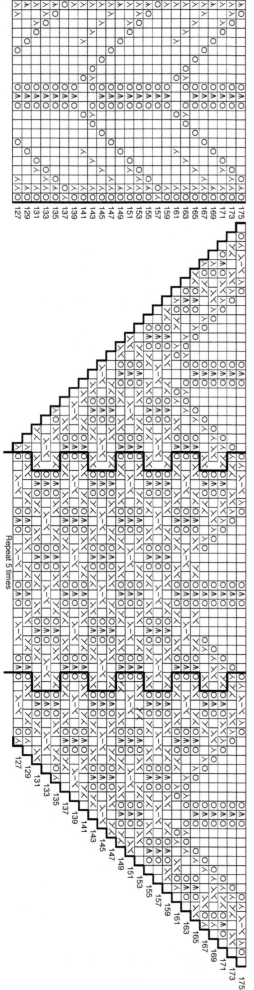

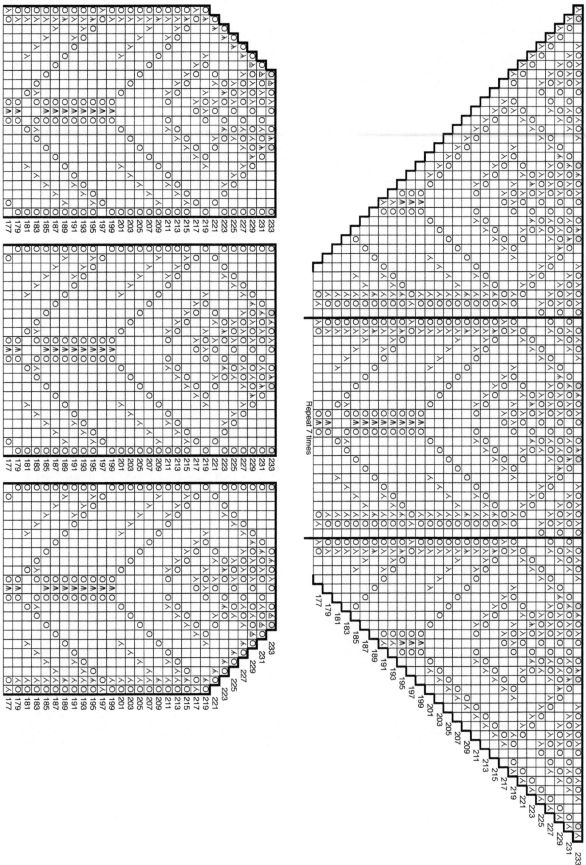

Mystic Roses – CHART F, right (small shawl only)

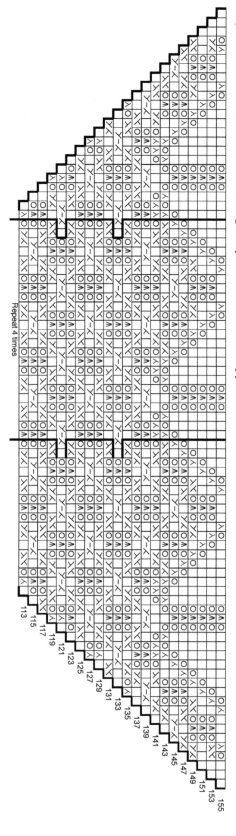

CHART F, left (small shawl only)

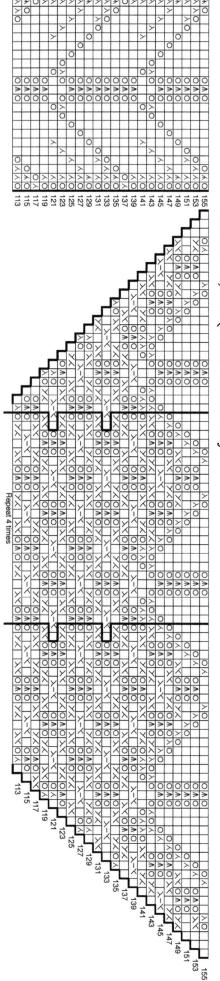

Mystic Roses – CHART G (small shawl only)

Repeat 6 times

mystic air

This square shawl is the fourth shawl in the Mystic Elements series (following Mystic Waters, Mystic Light and Mystic Earth). Mystic Air draws its inspiration from the heavens above and the air that we breathe.

When designing Mystic Air, I was considering different ways in which to create a square shawl. And then I decided to combine several of them.

In this shawl, first the center portion is knit as a straight square. Stitches are then picked up around the outside of the square, and the section with all the drops is worked in the round. Finally, the border is worked as a knit-on edging. This way, the knit rows are going in many different directions. Construction-wise, it's a fairly complex design, and it combines many different techniques, but following the pattern is not particularly difficult.

Before actually knitting Mystic Air, I of course had to wind the yarn—no small feat in this case. The yarn came in two 100 g skeins, each containing 1,200 m of laceweight yarn. Up until this point, I had always considered the time when I wound yarn a relaxing break from the knitting. It was almost meditative. But after winding 2,400 m of laceweight yarn by hand, my hands were cramping, and all thoughts of meditation had fled. I decided to invest in a yarn winder and have never regretted the purchase.

I was considering different ways in which to create a square shawl. And then I decided to combine several of them.

Mystic Air

MATERIALS

2 skeins TriCoterie Alpaca Cashsilk [70% baby alpaca, 20% silk, 10% cashmere; 1312 yds/1200 m per 100g skein] shown in Bella Swan

32 in length US 4 [3.5 mm] circular needle

47 or 60 in length US 4 [3.5 mm] circular needle

Large-eyed, blunt needle

Stitch markers, including one unique marker

GAUGE

16 sts and 34 rows = 4 in [10 cm] in stockinette, blocked

FINISHED (BLOCKED) SIZE

There are three possible sizes for Mystic Air. The blocked dimensions of the various sizes are:

Large size (original): 63 in [160 cm] square

Medium size: 55 in [140 cm] square

Small size: 49 in [124 cm] square

INSTRUCTIONS

Center Section (All Sizes)

CO 141 sts using a provisional cast on.

Rows 1–3: K141.
Row 4: K2, p137, k2.

Work charts A–E through row 269.

Note: Only RS rows are charted. All WS rows are: K2, p137, k2.

Row 270 (WS): K2, p137, k2.
Row 271: K141.

Row 272: K141. (Note: This is a good place to switch to a longer cord on your circular needle.)

Row 273: K141, place marker. This will mark the beginning of your new rounds, so it is convenient if this marker is different from the other markers.

Pick up and knit 141 sts along the left edge of the shawl. Place marker.

Pick up and knit 141 sts along the cast-on edge. Place marker.

Pick up and knit 141 sts along the right edge of the shawl. Place marker.

Knit 141 sts along the top of the shawl. (Now you are back to the marker for the beginning of the new rounds).

Knit one full round (564 sts).

Small size only: Skip to **Edging: Small Size.**

First Set of Raindrops (Medium and Large Only)

Work the next 36 rnds as follows:

» Odd-numbered rnds: [Corner chart 1, chart D] 4 times.

» Even-numbered rnds: Knit.

Medium size only: Skip to **Edging: Medium Size.**

Second Set of Raindrops (Large Only)

At this point, move the marker for the beginning of the rounds to be right after the column of yarn overs. The yarn over will continue to be the first stitch of the round. For the subsequent round, the yarn over will become the last stitch of the round.

Work rnds 37–72 as follows:

» Odd-numbered rnds: [Corner chart 2, chart E] 4 times.

» Even-numbered rnds: Knit.

At this point, you have 840 sts on your needles. Break the yarn. Then CO 14 sts using a provisional cast on.

Work row 17 of the edging chart and attach the last stitch of row 17 to the first stitch in the round of the shawl. Continue with rows 18–20 of the edging chart, attaching the edging to subsequent stitches in the last round knit on the square shawl (rnd 72).

EDGING

Large Size

Continue using the edging chart, knit rows 1–20 and rep 83 times. Then start an 84th rep and knit up to and including row 15.

Break the yarn and graft together with the cast-on side of the border starting at the main body of the shawl moving towards the outer edge. Sew in ends and block.

Medium Size

Knit the center section as written, and the first set of raindrops.

At this point, move the marker for the beginning of the rounds to be right after the column of yarn overs. The yarn over will continue to be the first stitch of the round.

For the subsequent round, the yarn over will become the last stitch of the round.

Rnd 37: [Yo, k33, yo, k143] 4 times (712 sts).
Rnd 38: Knit.

Rnd 39: [Yo, k33, yo, k145] 4 times (720 sts).
Rnd 40: Knit.

Break the yarn. Then CO 14 sts using a provisional cast on.

Knit row 17 of the edging chart and attach the last stitch of row 17 to the first stitch in the round of the shawl. Continue with rows 18–20 of the edging chart, attaching the edging to subsequent stitches in the last round knit on the square shawl.

Continue using the edging chart, knit rows 1–20 and rep 83 times Then start an 84th rep and knit up to and including row 15.

Break the yarn and graft together with the cast-on side of the border starting at the main body of the shawl moving towards the outer edge. Sew in ends and block.

Small Size

Knit the center section as written, including the instructions to pick up the stitches along the sides, place markers and knit one full round of 564 sts. After that, do NOT knit any of the raindrops.

Instead, knit the next 10 rows as follows:

Rnd 1: [Yo, k141] 4 times.
Rnd 2: Knit.

Rnd 3: [Yo, k1, yo, k141] 4 times.
Rnd 4: Knit.

Rnd 5: [Yo, k3, yo, k141] 4 times.
Rnd 6: Knit.

Rnd 7: [Yo, k5, yo, k141] 4 times.
Rnd 8: Knit.

Rnd 9: [Yo, k7, yo, k141] 4 times.
Rnd 10: Knit.

At this point you should have 600 sts on your needles.

Break the yarn. Then CO 12 sts using a provisional cast on.

Knit row 5 of the edging chart and attach the last stitch of row 5 to the first stitch in the round of the shawl. Continue with rows 6–20 of the edging chart, attaching the edging to subsequent stitches in the last round knit on the square shawl.

Continue using the edging chart, knit rows 1–20 and rep 59 times. On the 60th rep you will only knit rows 1–5. Break the yarn and graft together with the cast-on side of the border starting at the main body of the shawl moving towards the outer edge. Sew in ends and block.

Mystic Air – CHART A, right half
(continued on next page)

(Right half of chart A continues from here.)

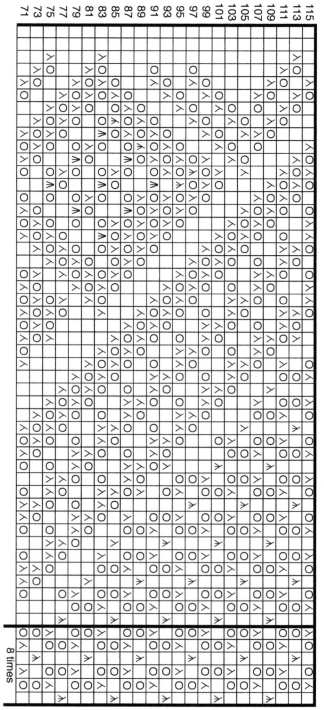

(Left half of chart B continues from here.)

Mystic Air – CHART B, right half

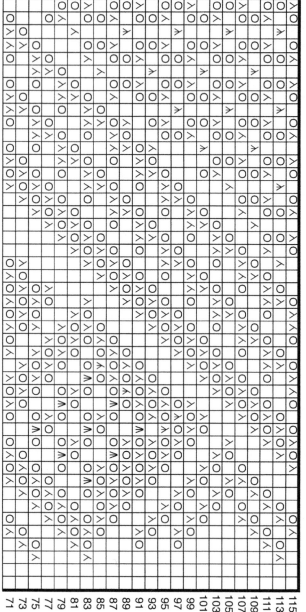

(Right half of chart B continues from here.)

8 times

Mystic Air – CHART C

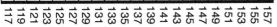
14 times

117 119 121 123 125 127 129 131 133 135 137 139 141 143 145 147 149 151 153 155 157

(Left half of chart D continues from here.)

Mystic Air – CHART D, left half

Mystic Air – CHART D, right half

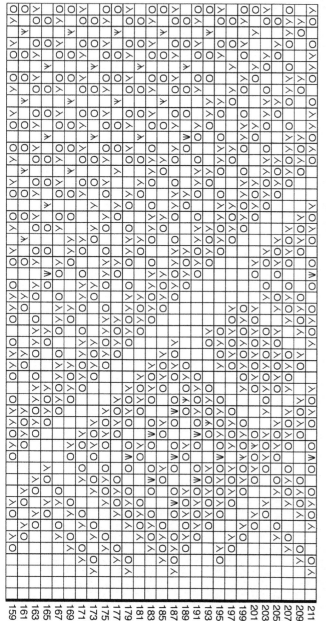

6 times

(Right half of chart D continues from here.)

(Left half of chart E continues from here.)

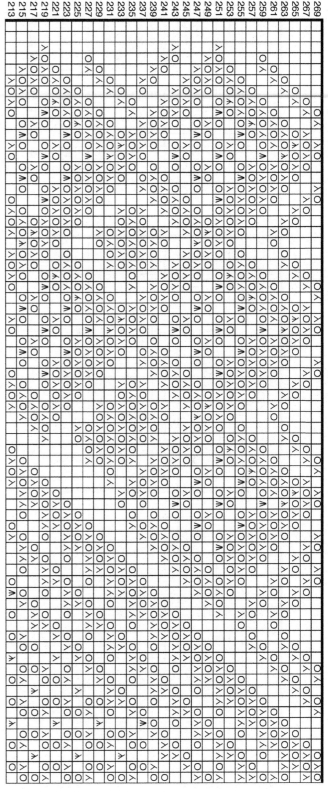

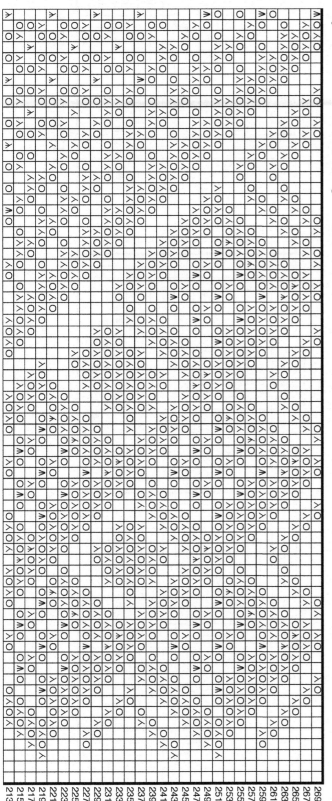

(Right half of chart E continues from here.)

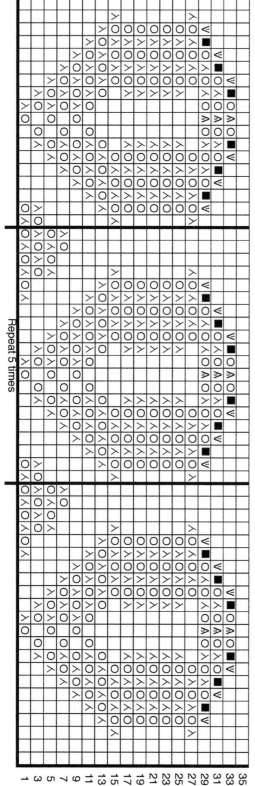

Mystic Air – CHART F

Repeat 5 times

Mystic Air – CHART G

Repeat 6 times

Mystic Air – CORNER CHART 1

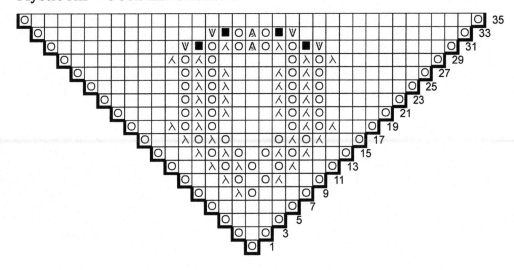

Mystic Air – CORNER CHART 2

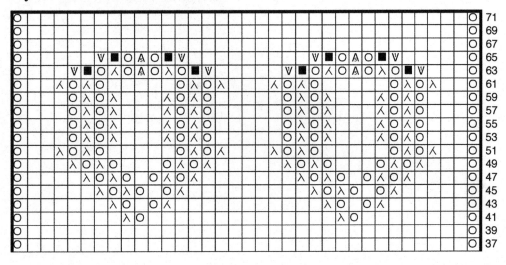

Mystic Air – EDGING CHART

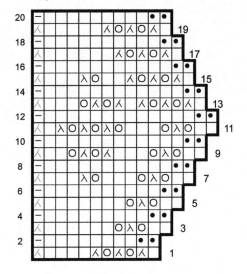

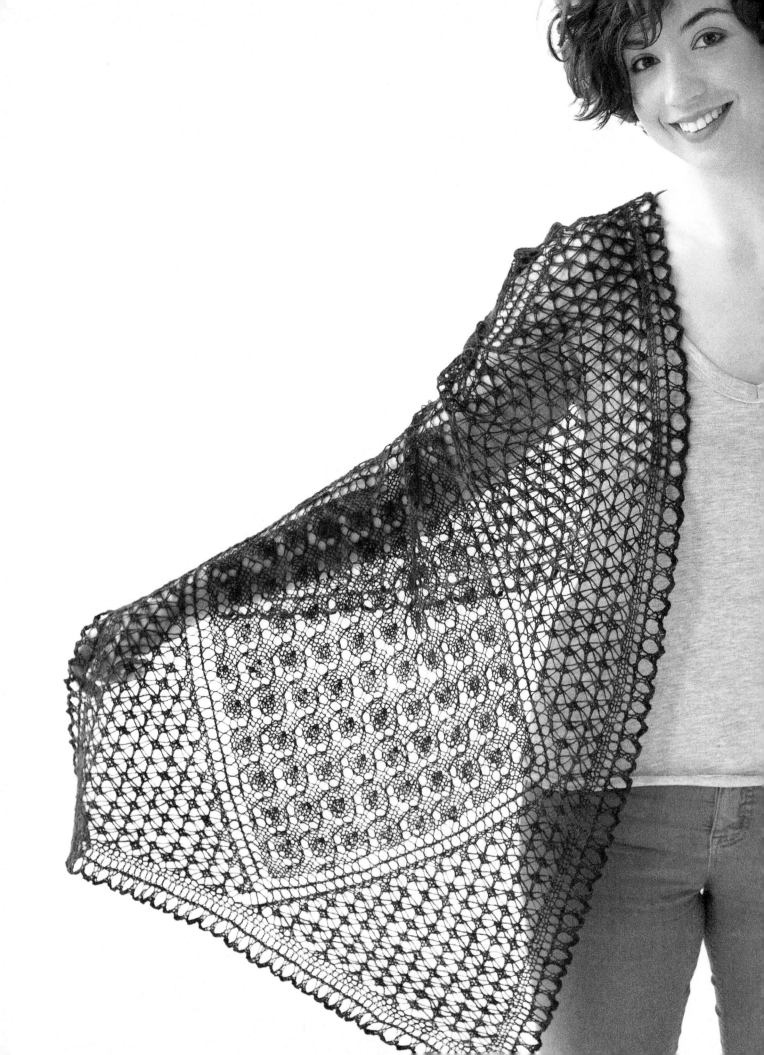

mystic embers

There is nothing more mesmerizing than the glowing embers in a burning fire. They capture your imagination like nothing else, and as you enjoy the dancing flames, the warmth envelops you like a cozy shawl.

Mystic Embers was designed during the summer, after I had spent many hours by the campfire. I've always been entranced by fires, and I can spend hours just gazing into them. So it was only natural to try to convey this in knitted form.

As a background pattern, I used an unusual lace pattern which is worked on a garter background with lace patterning on every row. The stitches themselves are fairly simple, but the resulting look is very textured and unusual. I then decided to divide the stole into thirds and on each third knit a diamond shape containing different types of flames.

The resulting shawl is very open and lacy, and in person it looks very textured.

Because there is lace patterning on both right-side and wrong-side rows, this is a fairly advanced pattern. It is absolutely critical to keep track of the place in the chart, and it can be tricky to fix mistakes after the fact.

I've always been entranced by fires, and I can spend hours just gazing into them. So it was only natural to try to convey this in knitted form.

Mystic Embers

1 skein of Mithril from Verdant Gryphon [100% merino – 750 yds/ 686 m per 113 g] in Rose Curculio or similar yarn

4.5 mm [US 7] needles

Large-eyed, blunt needle

GAUGE

13 sts and 22 rows = 4 in [10 cm] in pattern, blocked

FINISHED (BLOCKED) SIZE

length: 210 cm [83"], width: 72 cm [28"]

INSTRUCTIONS

CO 91 sts using a provisional cast on.

Begin working the charts in order, starting on row 1. Note that RS (odd-numbered) rows are read right to left, and WS (even-numbered) rows are read left to right.

After row 406, BO 2 sts. Replace stitch on ln.

EDGING CHART

Pick up the 91 sts from the provisional cast-on edge, and CO 5 sts using the knitted cast on. Turn work.

Edging row 1: K5, k2tog. Turn work.
Edging row 2: Sl1, k1, yo, k2tog, yo twice, k2. Turn work.

Continue edging by repeating the four rows in the edging chart below. When all stitches along the top of the stole have been used up, bind off the 8 stitches from the edging.

FINISHING INSTRUCTIONS

Sew in ends and block.

EDGING CHART

Mystic Embers – CHART A

113

Mystic Embers – CHART B

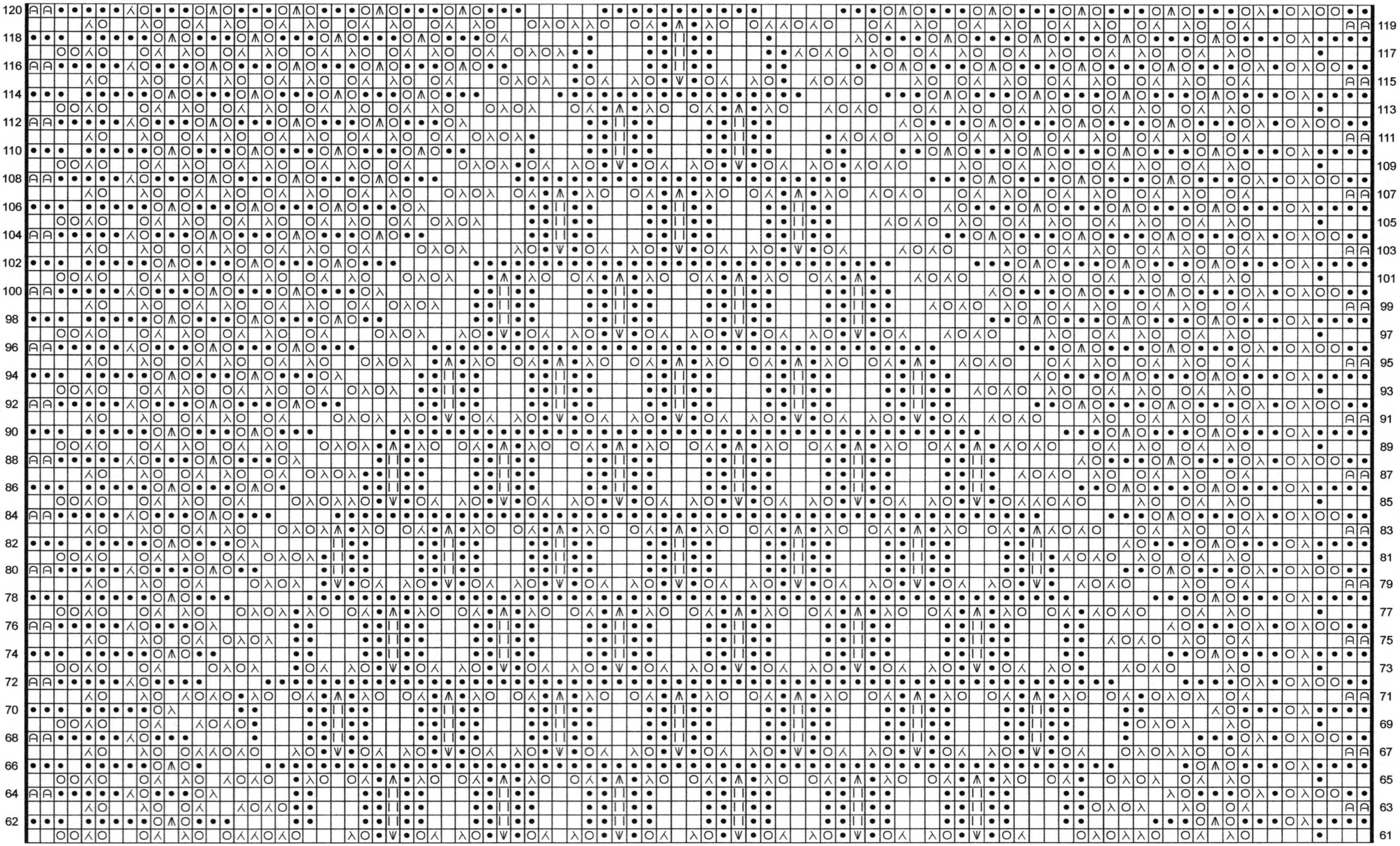

Mystic Embers – CHART C

Mystic Embers – CHART D

Mystic Embers – CHART E

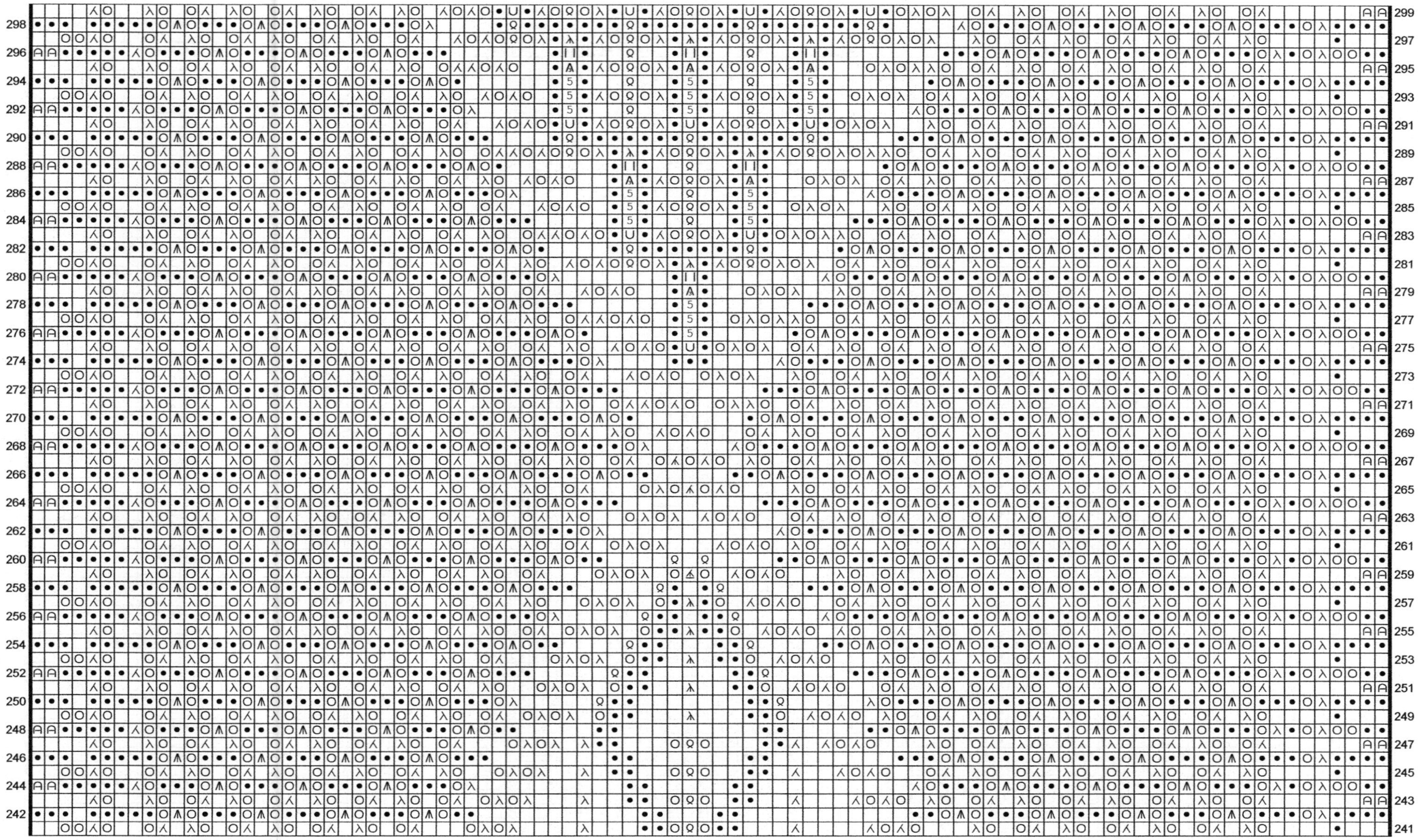

Mystic Embers – CHART F

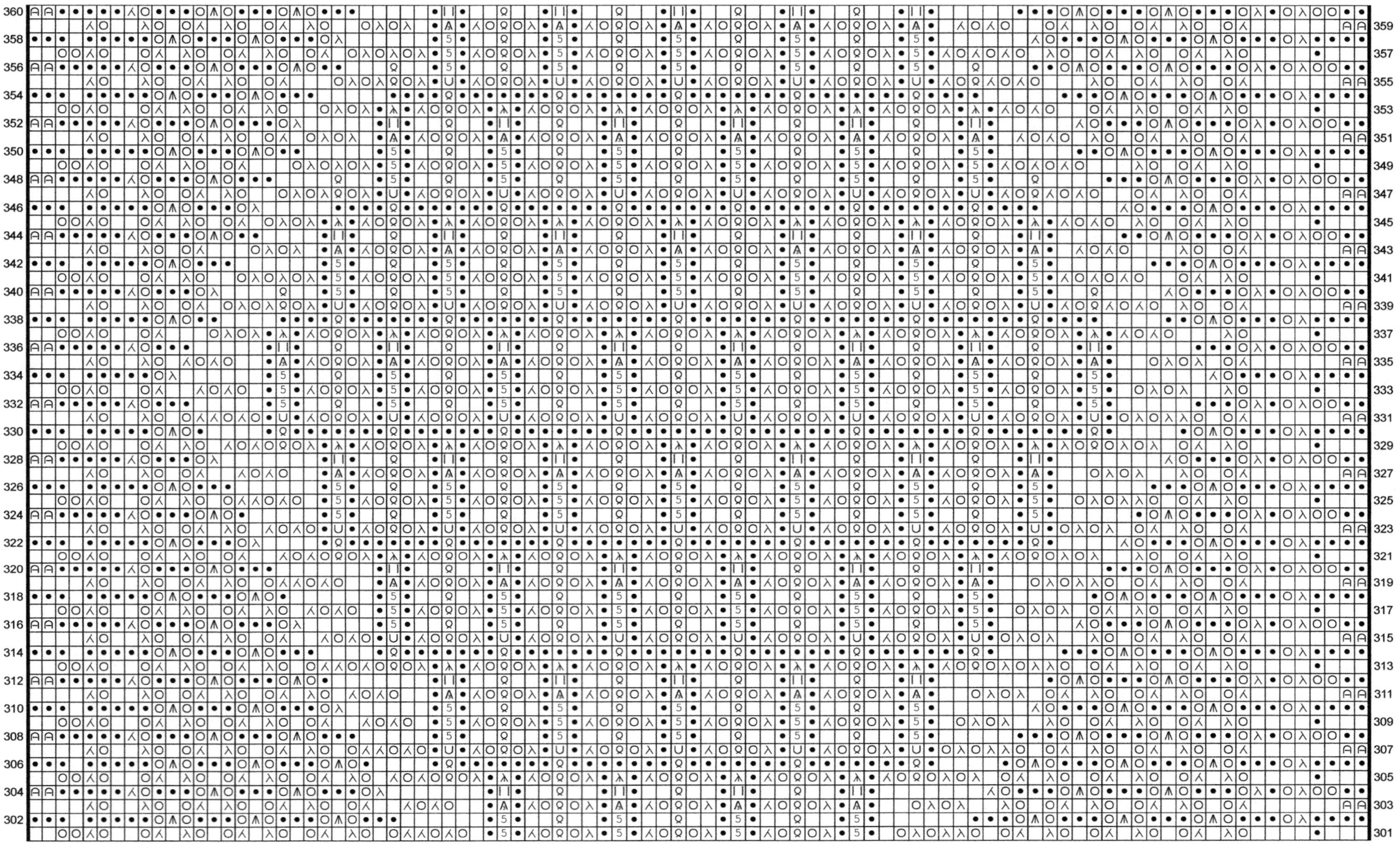

Mystic Embers – CHART G

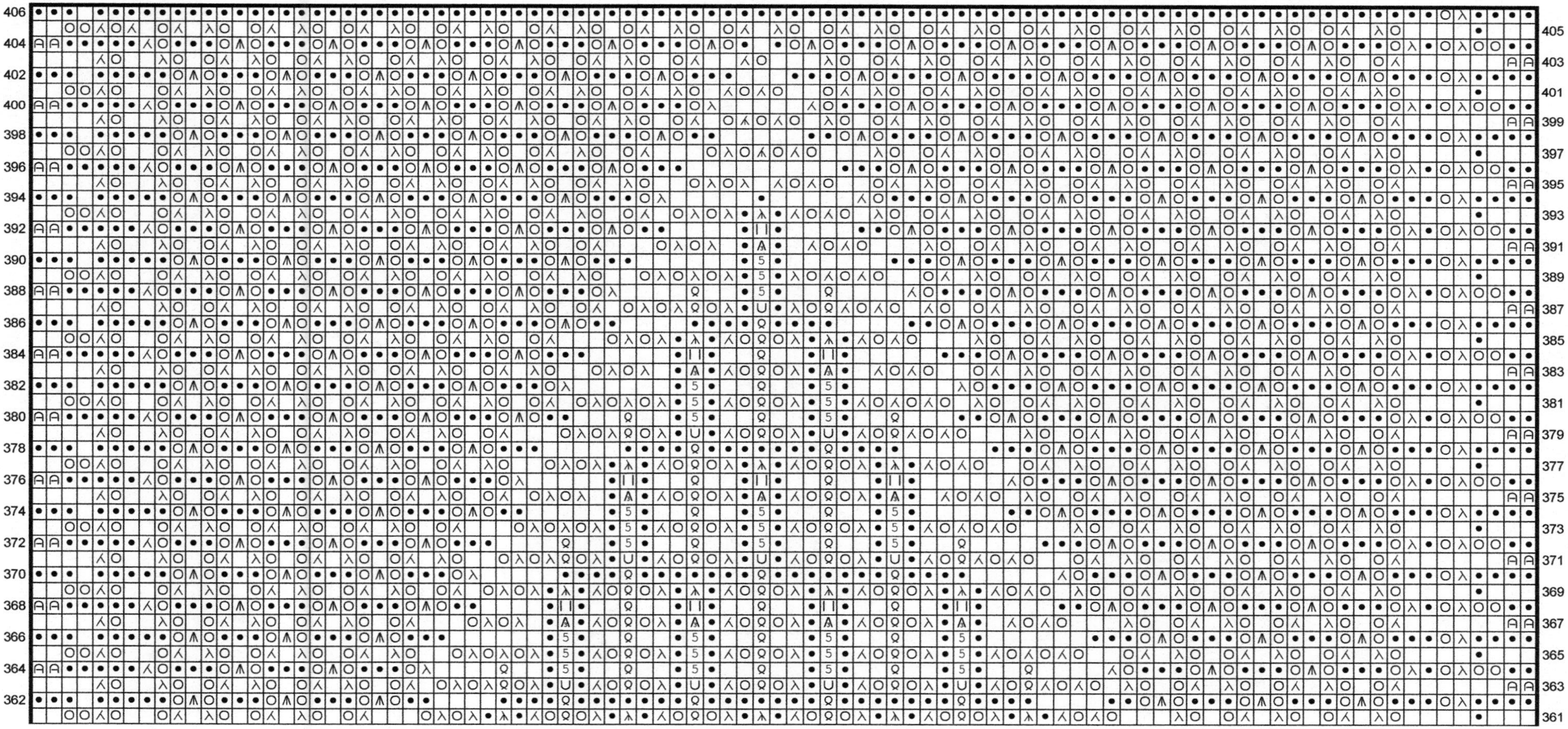

mystic diamonds

They say "Diamonds are Forever"—so for this stole I chose diamonds as a theme to symbolize everlasting love. To me, the glistening diamonds also mean beauty in the way they reflect the light.

Mystic Diamonds is a rectangular lace stole. The pattern is adjustable for both width and length.

The Mystic Diamonds KAL was my first knitalong to be hosted entirely on Ravelry. This changed the dynamic quite a bit, as people no longer had to use Yahoo groups to download the pattern. Instead, the pattern was distributed via an emailed download link, and it was easier to discuss the pattern in the Ravelry groups and include pictures directly in the posts. Because people were not on Ravelry solely to participate in the KALs, the discussions were more spread out than in the Yahoo groups.

Mystic Diamonds was designed as a wedding gift. I wanted a classic, clean look, and the shawl incorporates a number of different sized diamonds and clean, straight lines. It is worked in two halves that are then grafted together in the center. This makes the two sides perfectly symmetrical.

The edging is created by using a cabled cast on while holding the yarn double. The yarn overs and decreases then pull the fabric into a scalloped edge.

In order for the shawl to be maintain its symmetry with nupps in the center, the grafting unfortunately has to happen in a row with nupps. While the end result is lovely, had I designed this shawl today, I would have done something different on the last row to avoid this. For example, the nupp could have been replaced by a lacy hole (e.g. yo, followed by an ssk). Yes, this means that the diamonds in the center of the back would look slightly different from the rest on the shawl, but it would still be symmetrical and a *lot* simpler for the knitter.

Still, if diamonds are forever, then so is an intricately worked lace shawl, so perhaps we can suffer a little for our art.

I wanted a classic, clean look, and the shawl incorporates a number of different sized diamonds and clean, straight lines.

Mystic Diamonds

MATERIALS

3 skeins of Superwash Merino Lace by Tess' Designer Yarns [100% merino – 500 yds/457 m per 50 g] in teal or similar yarn

3.5 mm [US 4] needles

Large-eyed, blunt needle

GAUGE

17 sts and 32 rows = 4 in [10 cm] in pattern, blocked

FINISHED (BLOCKED) SIZE

Size adjustable

With 4 repeats: length: 204 cm [80"], width 75 cm [30"]

INSTRUCTIONS

This stole is worked in two halves, which are then grafted together. The width is adjustable.

The number of stitches to cast on is $31 + (X \times 24)$ where X equals the number of repeats you wish to include.

» For example, for 1 repeat (as written) you cast on $31 + (1 \times 24) = 55$ sts.

» With 4 repeats (as in the pictured sample) you cast on $31 + (4 \times 24) = 127$ sts.

First half of stole

** CO the required number of sts by using a knitted cast on and yarn held double.

Cut off one of the strands of yarn and weave in later. Continue knitting with one strand of yarn only.

Knit 2 rows, then start working the charts.

» Only RS rows are charted.

» Each WS row is worked: K2, purl to last 2 sts, k2.

After Chart A, continue with Chart B.

Rep rows 149–165 until you reach half the desired length of your stole. (I knit rows 149–165 a total of 4 times.) **

Then knit rows 167–169. Do not knit a WS row after row 169, but place all sts on a holder and set aside.

Second half of stole

Work as for the first half of the stole from ** to **.

Then knit row 167. Do not knit a WS row after row 167.

FINISHING INSTRUCTIONS

Graft the two pieces together using kitchener stitch. Be careful with the nupps, so that the grafting combines all 7 stitches from the nupp with one stitch on the other half.

Sew in ends and block.

Terry, Rogers City, MI

Mystic Diamonds – CHART A

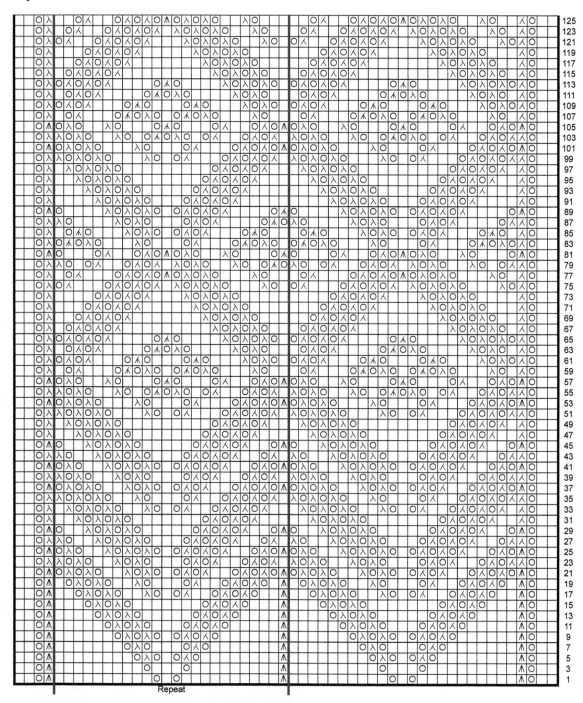

Repeat

Mystic Diamonds – CHART B

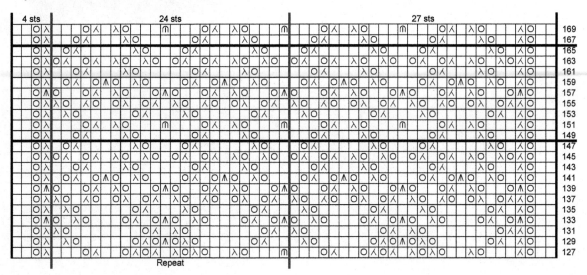

4 sts · 24 sts · 27 sts

Repeat

mystic desire

Black lace, a romantic fire, and perhaps two glasses of Champagne? Sound intriguing?

Sharpen your knitting needles and wind some lace yarn. At the end of this adventure, you will have a gorgeous lace shawl created by your dedicated work and your heart's desire. Then light your fire, bring out the champagne, and enjoy.

Mystic Desire is a triangular lace shawl knit from the top down. The shawl can be worked in two different sizes. It contains nupps, textured stitches, and various motifs often found in Estonian lace. Once again, I opted for a lace panel down the center spine, instead of just one knit spine stitch.

The yarn that I used came from Blue Moon Fiber Arts, and the colorway was part of their Raven Clan collection. The Raven Clan colors are a study in black—black that includes shades of other colors. It was a perfect choice for a mysterious, black shawl.

Rita Miller, Gonzales, LA

Mystic Desire

MATERIALS

1 skein of Laci from Blue Moon Fiber Arts [100% merino – 1750 yds/1600 m per 8 oz] in Thraven or similar yarn

3.75 mm [US 5] needles

Large-eyed, blunt needle

GAUGE

18 sts and 35 rows = 4 in [10cm] in stockinette stitch, blocked

FINISHED (BLOCKED) SIZE

Small version: width: 180 cm [71"], height: 90 cm [35.5"]

Large version: width 260 cm [102"], height: 130 cm [51"]

INSTRUCTIONS

CO 9 sts with a provisional cast on.

Work the setup chart (below).

Note: Only RS rows are charted. WS rows are k2, p7.

SETUP CHART

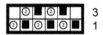

After working row 6, pick up 6 sts by purling them along the edge (right side of the chart), and then pick up 9 sts from the cast-on edge by purling the first 7 sts and knitting the last 2 sts.

At this point you will have 9+6+9=24 sts on your needles.

Setup row 7 (RS): K1, ssk, yo, k1, M2, M2, k1, yo, k1, M2, M2, k1, yo, k1, M2, M2, k1, yo, k2tog, k1.

Setup row 8 (WS): K2, purl to the last 2 sts, k2.

Turn and begin working the shawl pattern.

The rows are worked as follows:

» RS: K1, ssk, yo, edge chart, yo, charted row, yo, edge chart, yo, charted row, yo, edge chart, yo, k2tog, k1.

» WS: K2, purl to the last 2 sts, k2.

The edge chart (below) is a four-row chart (counting wrong sides) which is repeated.

EDGE CHART

For the large version of the shawl, work charts A–G.
In Chart F, work rep 6 times.
In Chart G, work rep 9 times.

For the small version of the shawl, work charts A–C, then skip to charts F–G.
In Chart F, work rep 4 times.
In Chart G, work rep 7 times.

FINISHING INSTRUCTIONS

Bind off as follows: K2, *return to ln, k2tog through back loop, k1, rep from * until no unworked sts remain.

Sew in ends and block. When blocking, pull the double tips of the edging to form points along the outer edge of the shawl.

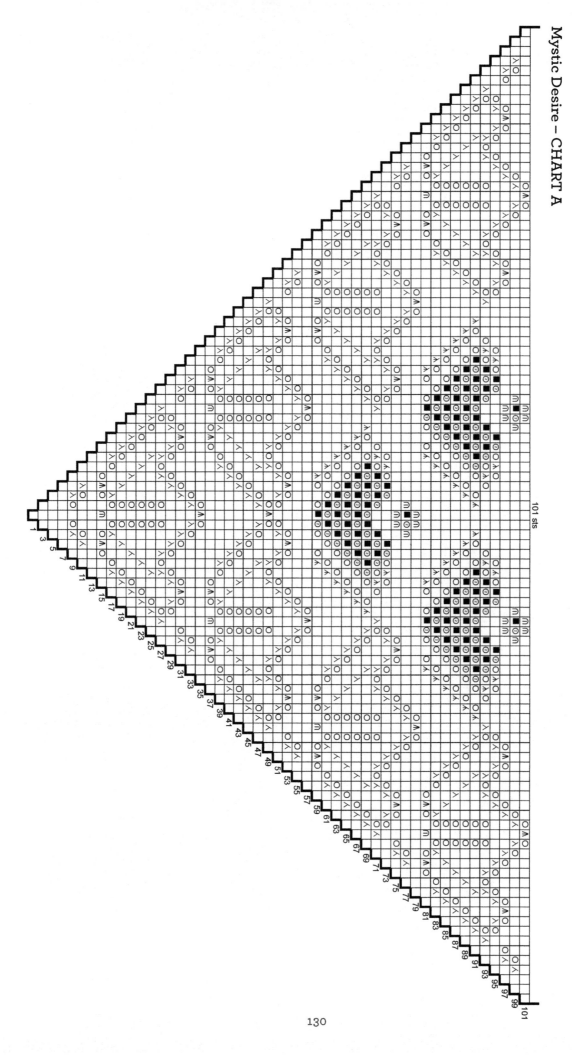

101 sts

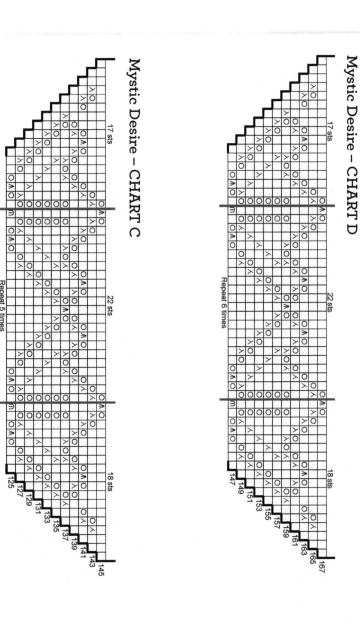

Mystic Desire – CHART B

Mystic Desire – CHART C

Mystic Desire – CHART D

131

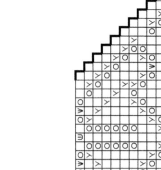

Mystic Desire – CHART F

Mystic Desire – CHART E

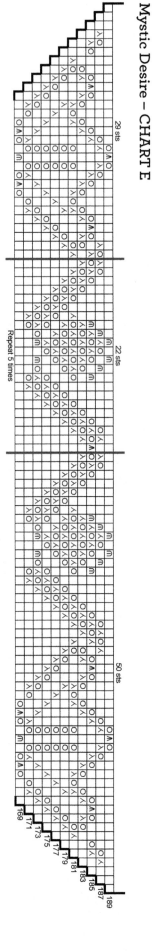

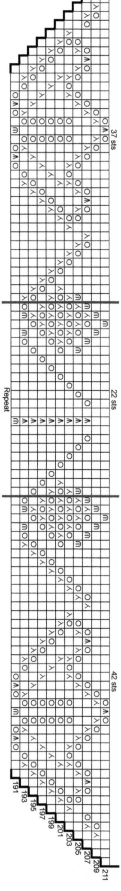

Mystic Desire – CHART G

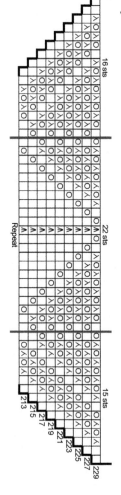

132

mystic midsummer wreath

Of all the nights during the year, Midsummer's Eve is the most magical and mystical. During that night, fairies dance and anything can happen. In Sweden, young girls pick seven different kinds of flowers in the hopes that they will dream of their true love.

People raise midsummer poles, fashion midsummer wreaths, and celebrate throughout the night, during which the sun doesn't set.

The Mystic Midsummer Wreath Shawl has a crescent shape, inspired by the midsummer wreaths worn by young and old on this magical day. (In the photo below, that's me wearing one of these wreaths.)

The shawl is constructed by casting on stitches along the bottom edge. By using a cabled cast on and the yarn held double, you create a thicker bottom edge. It's a technique often used in Estonian lace knitting and results in a nice, finished look.

Most of the motifs in this shawl are also inspired by Estonian lace motifs. The trefoil flowers along the edge use some unusual stitches.

Most crescent-shaped shawls that I had seen at this point had a solid body—either stockinette or garter stitch—but I wanted to use a lacy all-over pattern, and finish the look of the shawl with a lace edging both on the sides and across the top.

Mystic Midsummer Wreath

MATERIALS

2 skeins of Classic Merino Lace from Knitting Notions [100% merino wool – 385 yds/352 m per 50 g] in Dark Rose or similar yarn

4.0 mm [US 6] needles

Stitch markers

Large, blunt-tipped needle

GAUGE

18 sts and 36 rows = 4 in [10 cm] in stockinette stitch, blocked

FINISHED (BLOCKED) SIZE

Small size: wingspan: 178 cm [70"], height: 42 cm [17"]

Medium size: wingspan: 198 cm [78"], height: 45 cm [18"]

Large size: wingspan: 218 cm [86"], height: 48 cm [19"]

INSTRUCTIONS

CO 393 [429, 465] sts, using a cabled cast on and yarn held double. After working the cast on, cut off one of the strands of yarn and weave in later. Continue knitting with one strand of yarn only.

Work Chart A, repeating center section 20 [22, 24] times.

After row 38 on Chart A, there are 267 [291, 315] sts on the needles.

Begin Chart B:
Row 39: K3, p1, k4, k122, [134, 146], charted row 39.

Note: If you adjusted the shawl size to cast on a different number of stitches, row 39 is worked as follows:

Row 39: K3, p1, k3, knit to 2 sts before the center stitch, then work the charted row 39. The THIRD stitch of the charted row (a knit stitch) should be the center stitch of the shawl. That knit stitch should be centered on top of a double decrease from row 38.

Continue with chart B as written. Chart B is worked in short rows from the center out of the shawl.

Rows 45–52 are worked a total of SIX [SEVEN, EIGHT] times, each time adding 4 repeats of the section marked in red.

Then work rows 53–60 ONCE, repeating the highlighted section 21 [25, 29] times.

EDGING

Row 61: BO 2 sts, replace lone stitch on ln, then CO 7 sts using a cabled cast on.

Edge setup row: K7, k2tog, turn the work.

Work the edging chart perpendicular to the top edge of the shawl. Each k2tog at the end of rows 2 and 4 are worked together with a stitch from the top edge of the shawl.

Rep until no sts remain from body of shawl. Then turn and BO remaining 8 sts as follows: K2, *return to ln, k2tog through back loop, k1, rep from * until no unworked sts remain.

Above: Kirsten, Kolding, Denmark; Right: Valerie, Stoney Creek, ON, Canada

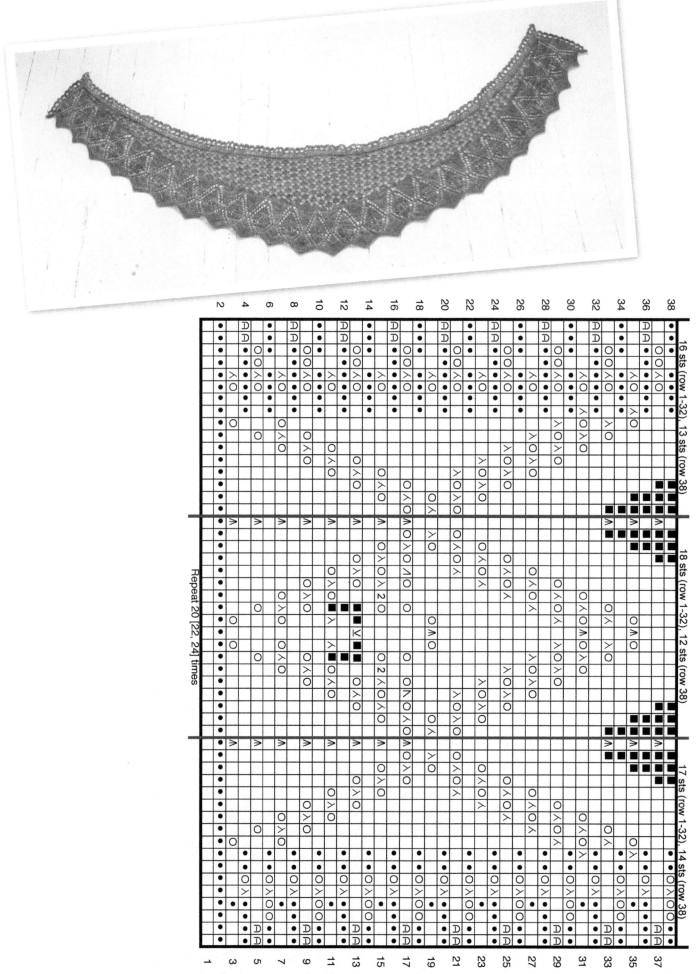

Mystic Midsummer Wreath – CHART A

16 sts (row 1-32), 13 sts (row 38)

18 sts (row 1-32), 12 sts (row 38)

17 sts (row 1-32), 14 sts (row 38)

Repeat 20 [22, 24] times

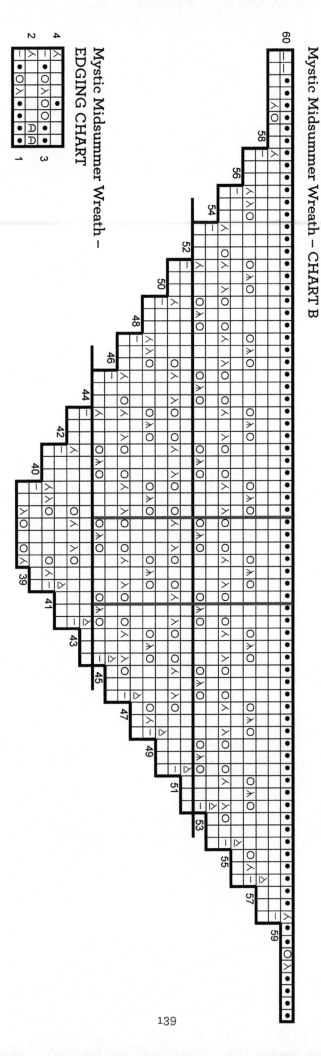

Mystic Midsummer Wreath –
EDGING CHART

139

mystic fire

Have you ever found yourself staring into a fire, captivated by the dancing flames? There is nothing more mesmerizing than a bonfire during the summer evenings.

Mystic Fire is a triangular shawl that draws its inspiration from the dancing flames in the summer bonfire. It starts with small flames against a stockinette background. Then it grows into larger flames that spread out across the entire body of the shawl and turn into the edging. Instead of a simple knit spine, there is lace patterning down the center of the shawl.

This design started with the yarn. Hazel Knits' Carnelian colorway reminded me of flames with its shades of yellow to red, which results in a vibrant orange look for the shawl.

The shawl is quite small compared to most of the Mystic shawls, because I wanted it to be a quick summer knit. The KAL ran through the month of June and the pattern was broken up into three parts, as opposed to most of the other Mystic KALs which have had 4-8 clues.

The funny thing with lace knitting is that a lot of the motifs can look like different things depending on how you look at them. During this KAL one person commented that the flames looked like angry birds to her. And while it had never occurred to me during the design process, or even while looking at the finished objects ... well....

One of my favorite ways to wear smaller shawls like Mystic Fire is to wrap it around my neck like a scarf (as shown on previous page). It's nice and warm under my winter coats, and looks nice as an accent with more plain shirts or dresses.

Mystic Fire

MATERIALS

1 skein of Divine from Hazel Knits [75% superwash merino, 15% cashmere, 10% silk – 400 yds/366 m per 115 g] in Carnelian or similar yarn

4.5 mm [US 7] needles

Large-eyed, blunt needle

GAUGE

13 sts and 29 rows = 4 in [10cm] in stockinette stitch, blocked

FINISHED (BLOCKED) SIZE

width: 148 cm [58"], height: 72 cm [28"]

INSTRUCTIONS

2-SECTIONED VERSION

Note: The orange sample shown in most of the photographs in this pattern is knit according to these instructions.

CO 2 sts using a provisional cast on.

Knit 10 rows.

K2, pick up and knit 5 sts along the side (one in each purl bump), pick up and knit 2 sts fro[m ...]
(9 sts).

Setup row 1 (RS): K[...] k1, yo, ssk, yo, k2.

Setup row 2 (WS): [...]

Then continue with the charts. Only the RS rows are charted. Rows are read from right to left.

Each RS row is worked: K2, yo, chart A, yo, center chart, yo, chart A, yo, k2. (When chart A is complete, insert chart B into sequence above.)

Each WS row is worked: K2, purl to the last 2 sts, k2.

Note: On rows 83 and 100 the four yarn overs in a row should be worked as p1, k1, p1, k1.

3-SECTIONED VERSION

Note: The coral sample pictured on 143 is knit according to these instructions.

CO 2 sts using a provisional cast on.

Knit 20 rows.

K2, pick up and knit 10 sts along the side (one in each purl bump), pick up and knit 2 sts from the CO edge (14 sts).

Setup row 1 (RS): K2, [yo, k2tog, yo, k1, yo, ssk] twice, yo, k2.

Setup row 2 (WS): K2, p10, k2.

Then continue with the charts. Only the RS rows are charted. Rows are read from right to left.

Each RS row is worked: K2, [yo, chart A, yo, center chart] twice, yo, chart A, yo, k2. (When chart A is complete, insert chart B into sequence above.)

Each WS row is worked: K2, purl to the last 2 sts, k2.

Note: On rows 83 and 100 the four yarn overs in a row should be worked as p1, k1, p1, k1.

COMPLETING THE SHAWL (BOTH VARIATIONS)

Rows 120–122: Knit.

Then bind off as follows: K2, *return to ln, k2tog through back loop, k1, rep from * until no unworked sts remain.

FINISHING INSTRUCTIONS

Sew in ends and block. When blocking, pull out the decreases to points.

3-sectioned variation of the shawl, Robin, Bellingham, WA

81 sts

1 3 5 7 9 11 13 15 17 19

69 71 73 75 77 79 81

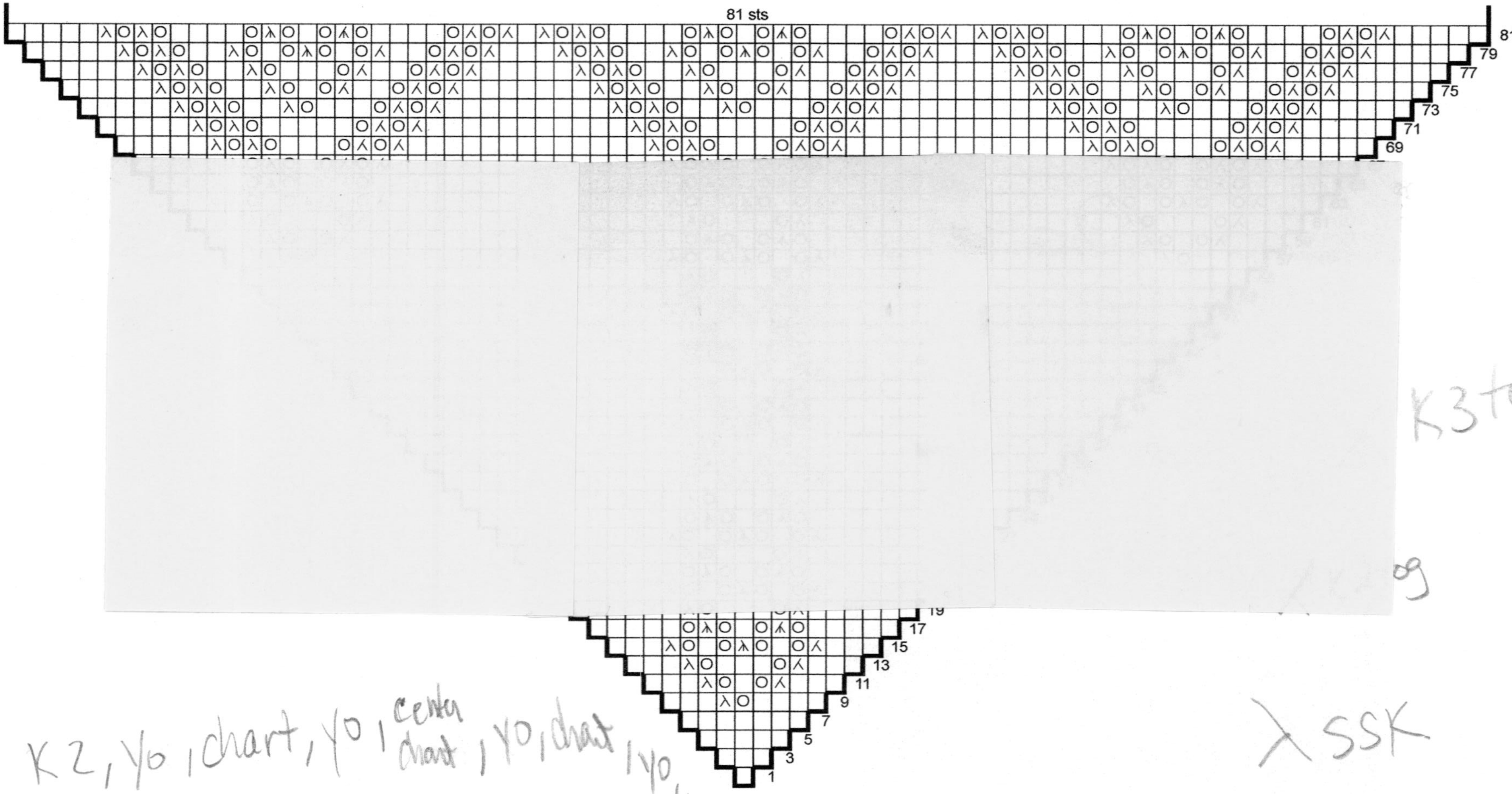

K2, yo, chart, yo, center, chart, yo, chart, yo, K2

K2, P1, K2

λ SSK

O yarn over

K3tog

8

9

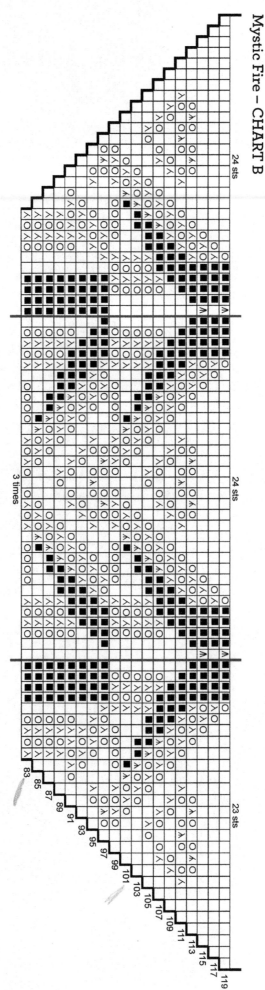

Mystic Fire – CHART B

145

mystic delight

Mystic Delight is a whimsical shawl, designed with bright and happy colors in mind.

I selected the colors on a dark and gray winter day, when I really just needed some color to cheer me up, and Tanis Fiber Arts' orange blossom and poppy colorways fit the bill perfectly. The final look of the shawl is greatly influenced by the colors chosen—bright combinations make it look cheerful, but it can become a classic, elegant shawl if you choose more conservative colors such as cream and charcoal.

This is the first Mystic shawl to use multiple colors in the design. Each section of the body is different but complementary, to add some variety to the knitting. There is a diamond pattern that goes from solid to nupps to lacy holes. It's easily memorizable, and a fairly relaxing knit.

The knitting finished with an intricate lace border that uses common lace stitches, twisted stitches, and separation between increases and decreases to create shifts in the fabric.

Jane, Brampton, ON, Canada

Mystic Delight

MATERIALS

1 skein of Red Label Cash Silk Single from Tanis Fiber Arts [75% merino, 15% cashmere, 10% silk – 420 yds/ 384 m per 115 g] in orange blossom or similar yarn

1 skein of Red Label Cash Silk Single from Tanis Fiber Arts [75% merino, 15% cashmere, 10% silk – 420 yds/384 m per 115 g] in poppy or similar yarn

3.75 mm [US 5] needles

Large-eyed, blunt needle

GAUGE

14 sts and 28 rows = 4 in [10 cm] in pattern, blocked

FINISHED (BLOCKED) SIZE

wingspan: 240 cm [94"],
height: 120 cm [47"]

INSTRUCTIONS

CO 5 sts using the cable cast on Setup row: K5.

Start working charts in order.

All RS rows: K2, charted row, k1, charted row, k2.

All WS rows: K2, charted row, p1, charted row, k2.

When working chart A, work rows 19–24 FOUR times, each time adding a rep of the sts in the red box. Then work rows 43–62.

When working chart B, work rows 63–68 FOUR times, each time adding a rep of the stis in the red box. Then work rows 87–110.

When working chart C, work rows 111–116 FOUR times, each time adding a rep of the sts in the red box. Then work rows 135–158.

When working chart D, work rows 159–193, repeating sts in the red box EIGHT times.

Row 194–196: Knit.

FINISHING INSTRUCTIONS

BO as follows: K2, *return to ln, k2tog tbl, k1, rep from * until no unworked sts remain.

Sew in ends and block.

Maria, Kansas City, MO

Mystic Delight – CHART A

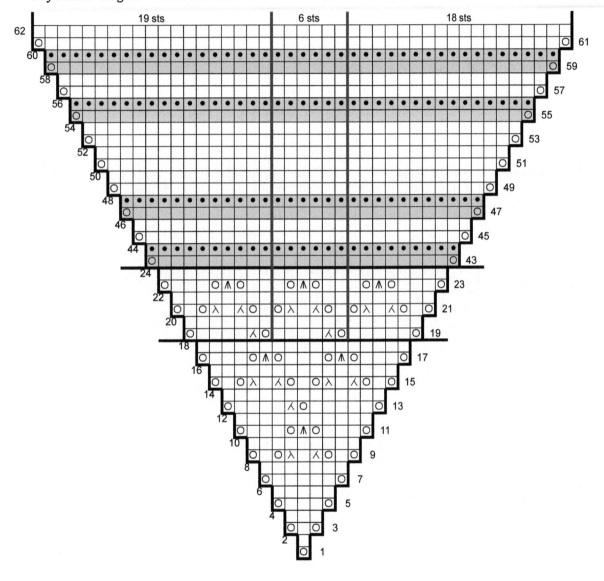

Note: The charts are color-coded; white stitches are knit in one color, gray in the other.

Mystic Delight – CHART B

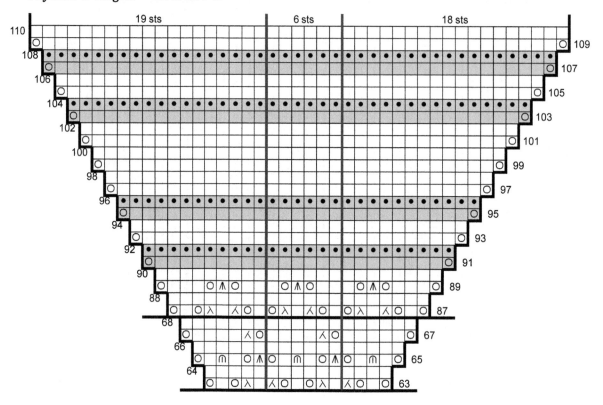

Mystic Delight – CHART C

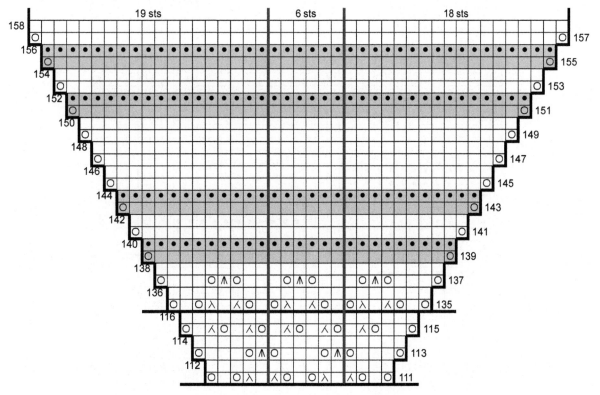

Mystic Delight – CHART D

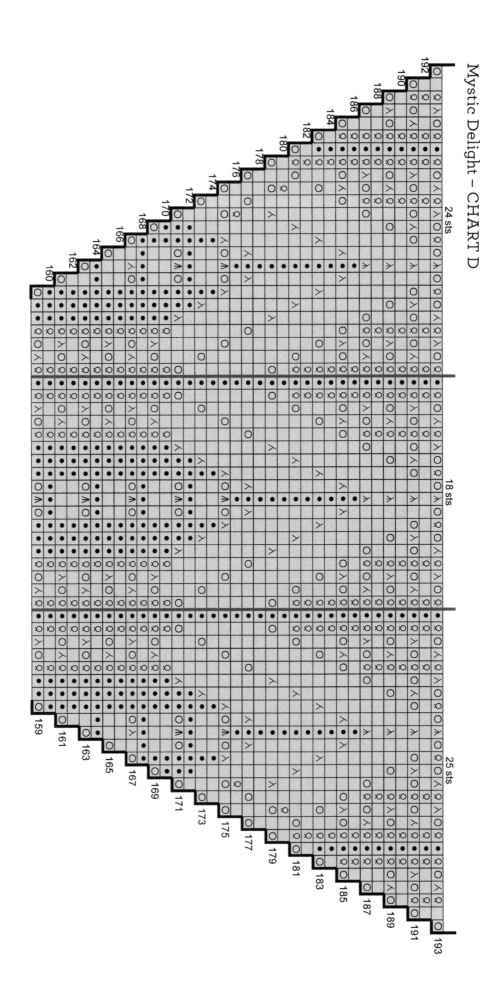

Abbreviations

BO – bind off

cn – cable needle

CO – cast on

C1B – slip 2 stitches onto a cable needle and hold behind the work, knit 1 stitch off the left hand needle, replace the leftmost stitch from the cable needle onto the left needle and knit that stitch, then knit the stitch off the cable needle

C1F – slip 2 stitches onto a cable needle and hold in front of the work, knit 1 stitch off the left hand needle, replace the leftmost stitch from the cable needle onto the left needle and knit that stitch, then knit the stitch off the cable needle

CB – slip 1 stitch onto cable needle, hold behind the work, k1 off left needle, k1 off cable needle

CF – slip 1 stitch onto cable needle, hold in front of work, k1 off left needle, k1 off cable needle

C2B – sl1 st onto cn, hold behind work, k1 off ln, k1 off cn

C2F – sl1 st onto cn, hold in front of work, k1 off ln, k1 off cn

C4F – sl2 sts onto cn, hold behind work, k2 off ln, k2 off cn

C4B – slip 2 stitches onto cable needle, hold behind work, k2 off left needle, k2 off cable needle

k – knit

kfb – knit in the front and the back of the stitch

ktbl – knit through the back loop

k2tog – knit 2 stitches together

k3tog – knit 3 stitches together

k4tog – knit 4 stitches together

ln – left needle

MB – make bobble as follows: [k, p, k, p] into one st, turn work and k4, turn work, sl 1, sl 1, k2tog, pass both slipped sts over

M2 – make 2 sts out of 2 by k2tog, and ktbl in the same stitch

M3 – [k, p, k] all into the same stitch

M5 – [k, p, k, p, k] all into the same stitch

nupp – [K, yo] 3 times, k all into the same stitch. Note: All 7 nupp stitches are purled together on the subsequent WS row.

p – purl

ptbl – purl through the back loop

psso – pass slipped stitch(es) over

p2tog – purl 2 stitches together

rep – repeat

rn – right needle

RS – right side

sl – slip

ssk – slip stitch as if to knit, slip stitch as if to knit, replace on left needle and knit both stitches together through the back loop

ssp – slip stitch as if to knit, slip stitch as if to knit, replace on left needle and purl both stitches together through the back loop

st(s) – stitch(es)

Symbol Guide & Special Symbols

wrap3 – [K2, p1, k2] onto cn. Pass yarn in front of all sts and then behind all the sts. (You have now wrapped the yarn once around all the sts.) Wrap the yarn two more times around the sts for a total of 3 wraps. Place the wrapped sts on rn.

wrap5 – K2 onto cn. Pass yarn in front of all sts and then behind all the sts. (You have now wrapped the yarn once around all the sts.) Wrap the yarn four more times around the sts for a total of 5 wraps. Place the wrapped sts on rn.

WS – wrong side

w5tog – work 5 sts together: ssk, k3tog, pass previous st (from ssk) over)

yo – yarn over

7×3 – seven from three stitches: slip 2 sts together (knitwise), knit 1 stitch, pass slipped sts over, in same stitch as double decrease [yo,k] 3 times for a total of 7 stitches

□	k on RS, p on WS
•	p on RS, k on WS
Ω	ktbl on RS, ptbl on WS
⋏	k2tog
⋏	k3tog
⟁	k4tog
λ	ssk
△	k2tog on WS
λ	sl1, k2tog, psso
⋀	slip 2 stitches together (knitwise), k1, pass slipped stitches over
⟁	p3tog
⋔	nupp
○	yarn over
■	no stitch
⊓	BO
—	sl1

Mystic Desire

②	M2

Mystic Embers

⋏	k2tog on RS, ssk on WS
❘ ❘	k3 on RS, p3 on WS
Å	k5 on RS, p5 on WS
V	M3
5	M5
A	decrease 5 sts to 3 by ssk, k1, k2tog

Mystic Earth

⋏	k2tog on RS, p2tog on WS
△	k2tog on WS
λ	ssk on RS, ssp on WS

Special Symbols (continued)

Mystic Light

⋏ k2tog on RS, p2tog on WS

Ѧ w5tog

Ѵ kfb

Mystic Meadows

⋏ k2tog on RS, ssk on WS

△ p2tog

⋋ ssk on RS, k2tog on WS

◿ ssp

⋋⋌ C2F

⋋ ⋌ C4F

Ξ MB

WRAP wrap3

W5 wrap5

MB – make bobble

Mystic Midsummer Wreath

⋏ k2tog on RS, ssk on WS

⋋ ssk on RS, k2tog on WS

◿ ssp on WS

⋀ slip 2 stitches together (knitwise), k2tog, pass slipped stitches over

⋀ slip 3 stitches together (knitwise), knit 1 stitch, pass slipped stitches over

Ѧ sl1, k3tog, psso

2 k2

⩔ 7×3

Mystic Roses

◿ k4tog

◿ sl1, k3tog, psso

⋎–⋌ C1B

⋋–⋌ C1F

⋎⋌ CB

⋋⋌ CF

Mystic Star

⋋ (symbol in blue) – start round 1 stitch early, then work a ⋋

About Anna

Anna Dalvi has been publishing knitting patterns online since 2007. She has published more than 100 patterns over the past several years. Her most popular designs are the Mystic lace shawls, originally published in a mystery knitalong format, which have attracted more than 7,000 knitters worldwide. This is her third book with Cooperative Press, following *Shaping Shawls* (2011) and *Ancient Egypt in Lace and Color* (2012).

In her knitting, Anna enjoys variety more than anything else—from intricate lace to sprawling cables, and differences in color and texture.

Anna is originally from Sweden, but has since moved to Ottawa, Canada. Anna holds a B.S. in Computer Science from Cornell University, and an M.B.A. from Queen's University.

She still hosts KALs on a regular basis. The latest KAL info is always available at knitandknag.com/kals, while the chit-chat and photo sharing tends to happen in the Knit & Knag Designs group on Ravelry (http://www.ravelry.com/groups/knit--knag-designs).

About Cooperative Press

Cooperative Press (formerly anezka media) was founded in 2007 by Shannon Okey, a voracious reader as well as writer and editor, who had been doing freelance acquisitions work, introducing authors with projects she believed in to editors at various publishers.

Although working with traditional publishers can be very rewarding, there are some books that fly under their radar. They're too avant-garde, or the marketing department doesn't know how to sell them, or they don't think they'll sell 50,000 copies in a year.

5,000 or 50,000. Does the book matter to that 5,000? Then it should be published.

In 2009, Cooperative Press (cooperativepress.com) changed its named to reflect the relationships we have developed with authors working on books. We work together to put out the best quality books we can and share in the proceeds accordingly.

Thank you for supporting independent publishers and authors.

ALSO FROM ANNA DALVI
AND COOPERATIVE PRESS

Shaping Shawls
Ancient Egypt in Lace and Color

CPSIA information can be obtained at www.ICGtesting.com
Printed in the USA
LVOW02s1229160715

446472LV00002B/3/P